P9-AGK-973

NATIONAL GEOGRAPHIC
Reach
for Reading
COMMON CORE PROGRAM

NATIONAL GEOGRAPHIC LEARNING | CENGAGE Learning

Acknowledgments

Grateful acknowledgment is given to the authors, artists, photographers, museums, publishers, and agents for permission to reprint copyrighted material. Every effort has been made to secure the appropriate permission. If any omissions have been made or if corrections are required, please contact the Publisher.

Cover Design and Art Direction: Visual Asylum

Cover illustration: Joel Sotelo

Illustration Credits: All PM illustrations by National Geographic Learning.

For product information and technology assistance, contact us at
Customer & Sales Support, 888-915-3276

For permission to use material from this text or product, submit all requests online at **www.cengage.com/permissions**
Further permissions questions can be emailed to
permissionrequest@cengage.com

National Geographic Learning | Cengage Learning
1 Lower Ragsdale Drive
Building 1, Suite 200
Monterey, CA 93940

Cengage Learning is a leading provider of customized learning solutions with office locations around the globe, including Singapore, the United Kingdom, Australia, Mexico, Brazil, and Japan. Locate your local office at **www.cengage.com/global**.

Cengage Learning products are represented in Canada by Nelson Education, Ltd.

Visit National Geographic Learning online at **NGL.Cengage.com**
Visit our corporate website a **www.cengage.com**

Printed in the USA.
Globus Printing, Minster, OH

ISBN: 978-13054-98990 (Practice Book)

ISBN: 978-13056-58691 (Practice Masters)

Teachers are authorized to reproduce the practice masters in this book in limited quantity and solely for use in their own classrooms.

Printed in the United States of America

17 18 19 20 21 22 23 24

13 12 11 10 9 8 7

Contents

Unit 1: My Family

Unit 2: Shoot for the Sun

Unit 3: To Your Front Door

Unit 4: Growing and Changing

Name _____ Date _____

Letter and Sound Mm

Write the missing letter. Color each item named in the sentence.

1. ___op **m**op	**2.** ___an	**3.** ___ask
4. ___ouse	**5.** ___ilk	**6.** ___itt
7. ___oon	**8.** ___at	**9.** ___ap

Read It Together   Find the man and the mat.

For use with TE p. T3c   **PM1.1**   Unit 1 | My Family

Name _____ Date _____

Phonics

Letter and Sound Ss  Ss

Write the missing letter. Color each item named in the sentence.

1. _s_oap	**2.** __ilk	**3.** __un
4. __ink	**5.** __eed	**6.** __ock
7. __eal	**8.** __ix	**9.** __even

Read It Together   Find the sun and the six.

For use with TE p. T3c   **PM1.2**   **Unit 1 | My Family**

Name _____ Date _____

Letter and Sound Hh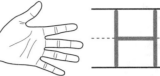

Write the missing letter. Color each item named in the sentence.

1. ___hat	**2.** ___ook	**3.** ___un
4. ___ask	**5.** ___an	**6.** ___ose
7. ___and	**8.** ___ouse	**9.** ___orn

Read It Together   Find the hat and the hand.

PM1.3   Unit 1 | My Family

Phonics

Letter and Sound Tt

Write the missing letter. Color each item named in the sentence.

1. ten	**2.** itt	**3.** ape
4. ock	**5.** ub	**6.** ire
7. orse	**8.** op	**9.** able

Read It Together   Find the ten and the tub.

Name _____ Date _____

High Frequency Words

Trace each word two times and then write it.

find find find

has has has

have have have

his his his

mother mother mother

too too too

Cut out the pictures and the book. Fold the book on the solid lines. Paste an *m* picture on each page and write its name. Read the sentence and color what it names.

Read It Together

Find the man.

My M m Book

Name _____ Date _____

Cut out the pictures and the book. Fold the book on the solid lines.
Paste an *s* picture on each page and write its name. Read the
sentence and color what it names.

Read It Together

Find the Sun.

My S s Book

Name _____ Date _____

Cut out the pictures and the book. Fold the book on the solid lines. Paste an *h* picture on each page and write its name. Read the sentence and color what it names.

My H h Book

Read It Together

Find the hat.

Cut out the pictures and the book. Fold the book on the solid lines. Paste a *t* picture on each page and write its name. Read the sentence and color what it names.

Read It Together

My T t Book

Find the tub.

High Frequency Word Cards

a	find
am	has
I	have
is	his
like	mother
my	too

Name _____   Date _____

Organize Ideas

Write about what your family does together.

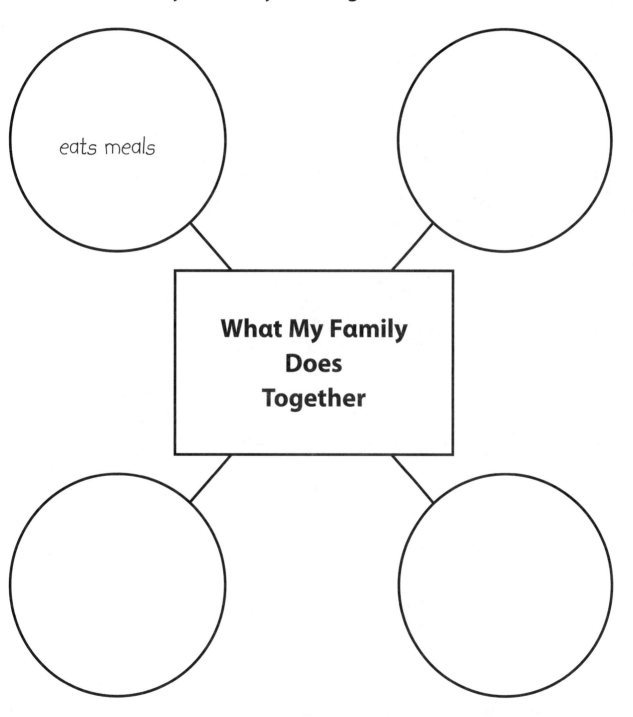

eats meals

What My Family Does Together

Name _____ Date _____

Letter and Sound Aa

Write the missing letter. Color the item named in the sentence.

1. apple	**2.** op
3. x	**4.** ox
5. lligator	**6.** nt

Read It Together Find the ax.

Name _____ Date _____

Find a Hat

Write a word from the box to complete each sentence.

High Frequency **Words**
find
has
have
his
mother
too

_____

1. Sam _____ a hat.

_____

2. _____ hat is on the mat.

_____

3. His _____ sat on his hat!

_____

4. I have a hat, _____ .

_____

5. _____ my hat!

Grammar: Nouns

Use Nouns

1. Play Tic Tac Toe. Point to a square.

2. Say the word. Tell whether it names one or more than one person, place, or thing.

3. Use the word in a sentence.

4. If you choose the middle square, name your own noun. Complete steps 2 and 3.

5. Place your game marker in the square.

child	feet	woman
foot	Draw a noun. Name it.	men
man	women	children

Name _____ Date _____

Cut out the pictures and the book. Fold the book on the solid lines.
Paste an *a* picture on each page and write its name. Read the
sentence and color what it names.

Read It Together

My A a Book

Find the ant.

Grammar and Writing

Write Nouns

Singular Nouns	Plural Nouns
child	children
brother	brothers
house	houses

Read each sentence. Find a word from the word bank that completes the sentence. Write the word in the sentence.

1. My mom and dad are my (parent/parents).

2. They have two (child/children).

3. I have one (brother/brothers).

4. We live in a (house/houses).

5. We play many (game/games).

6. I love my (family/families).

Name _____ Date _____

Yes or No?

1. Listen to the questions. Write the Key Word where it belongs in each sentence.

2. Listen to the questions again.

3. Check Yes or No for each question.

	Yes	No

1. Is breakfast a ____meal____ ?   ☑ ☐

2. Is a teacher a _____ ?   ☐ ☐

3. Can an apartment be a _____ ?   ☐ ☐

4. Is New Year's Day a _____ ?   ☐ ☐

5. Can you _____ a birthday?   ☐ ☐

6. Is a group of students a _____ ?   ☐ ☐

Name _____ Date _____

Families in Many Cultures

Write about what families do together.

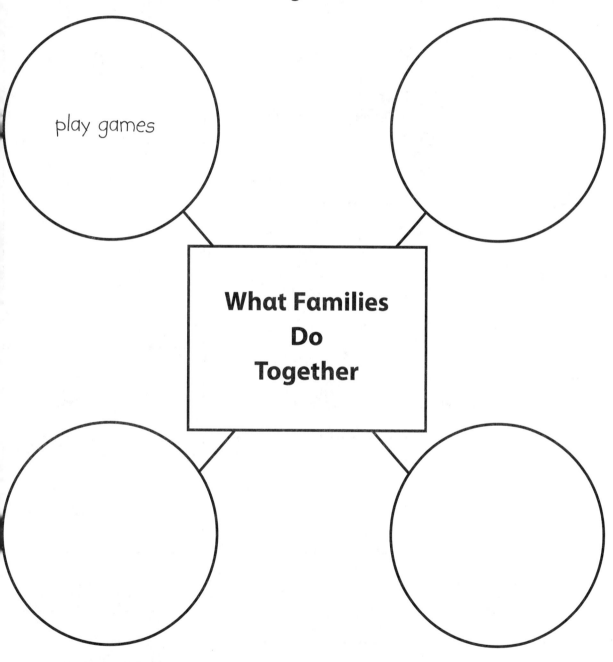

play games

What Families Do Together

Read It Together Take turns with a partner. Tell what you learned about families in "Families in Many Cultures."

Name _____ Date _____

Letter and Sound Ff

Ff

Write the missing letter. Color each item named in the sentence.

1. f ox	**2.** ink	**3.** ork
4. ence	**5.** an	**6.** ive
7. oot	**8.** ish	**9.** ire

Read It Together   Find the fan and the fox.

For use with TE p. T23o   **PM1.19**   Unit 1 | My Family

Name _____   Date _____

Letter and Sound Nn

Nn

Write the missing letter. Color each item named in the sentence.

1. __nut	**2.** __en	**3.** __ine
4. __op	**5.** __ail	**6.** __est
7. __et	**8.** __ose	**9.** __ox

Read It Together   Find a nut and a net.

Name _____   Date _____

Phonics

Letter and Sound Ll

Write the missing letter. Color each item named in the sentence.

1. ___ eg	**2.** ___ ub	**3.** ___ emon
4. ___ eaf	**5.** ___ ape	**6.** ___ amb
7. ___ orn	**8.** ___ og	**9.** ___ amp

Read It Together   Find the leg and the log.

Name _____ Date _____

Letter and Sound Pp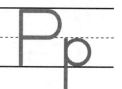

Write the missing letter. Color each item named in the sentence.

1. ___pen	**2.** ___at	**3.** ___an
4. ___ear	**5.** ___eas	**6.** ___un
7. ___ire	**8.** ___illow	**9.** ___ot

Read It Together   Find the pan and the pot.

Name _____ Date _____

Letter and Sound Cc

Cc

Write the missing letter. Color each item named in the sentence.

1. ___cat	**2.** ___up	**3.** ___ix
4. ___an	**5.** ___ap	**6.** ___oot
7. ___ouse	**8.** ___orn	**9.** ___ow

Read It Together   Find the cat and the cap.

Grammar

Choose A or An

holiday	brother	egg
apple	friend	grandfather
sister	home	uncle
bed	orange	table
aunt	parent	meal
grandmother	banana	sister

Handwriting

High Frequency Words

Trace each word two times and then write it.

do do do

then then then

what what what

with with with

you you you

your your your

Name _____ Date _____

Cut out the pictures and the book. Fold the book on the solid lines.
Paste an *f* picture on each page and write its name. Read the
sentence and color what it names.

Read It Together

My F f Book

Find the fan.

Name _____ Date _____

Cut out the pictures and the book. Fold the book on the solid lines.
Paste an *n* picture on each page and write its name. Read the
sentence and color what it names.

Read It Together

Find the nap.

My N n Book

Name _____ Date _____

Cut out the pictures and the book. Fold the book on the solid lines. Paste an *l* picture on each page and write its name. Read the sentence and color what it names.

Read It Together

My L l Book

Find the lamp.

Name _____ Date _____

Cut out the pictures and the book. Fold the book on the solid lines. Paste a *p* picture on each page and write its name. Read the sentence and color what it names.

Read It Together

Find the pan.

My P p Book

Cut out the pictures and the book. Fold the book on the solid lines. Paste a *c* picture on each page and write its name. Read the sentence and color what it names.

Read It Together

Find the can.

My C c Book

High Frequency Word Cards

and	do
little	then
that	what
the	with
this	you
on	your

Name _____ Date _____

Compare Authors' Purposes

Compare "Families in Many Cultures" and "The World Is Your Family."

"Families in Many Cultures"	"The World Is Your Family"
to show families in different places	

Read It Together   Take turns with a partner. Tell how the authors' purposes are different.

Name _____ Date _____

Letter and Sound Ii

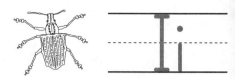

Write the missing letter. Color each item named in the sentence.

1. insect	**2.** all
3. pple	**4.** gloo
5. ll	**6.** even

Read It Together Find the insect and the igloo.

Name _____ Date _____

Find Nat!

Write a word from the box to complete each sentence.

High Frequency **Words**
do
then
what
with
you
your

_____

1. Can _____ find Nat the cat?

_____

2. Is Nat on the mat _____ Pam?

_____

3. _____ is that in the cap?

_____

4. Nat, _____ you like to nap?

_____

5. _____ you can nap in your cap!

PM1.34

Name _____ Date _____

Cut out the pictures and the book. Fold the book on the solid lines. Paste an _i_ picture on each page and write its name. Draw a picture to go with the sentence.

My I i Book

Read It Together

Draw a wig on a pig.

Grammar and Writing

Write Articles and Plural Nouns

1. Read the story.

2. Circle the correct articles.

3. Fill in the blanks with plural nouns. Add *-s* or *-es*.

It takes a lot of work to make (a/the) garden! First,

we cleaned up (a/the) yard. Then we moved two

_____

_____ (bench) near the garden. Next, we

_____

bought some seeds. I got _____ (bean) and

_____

_____ (sunflower). I also got (a/an)

apple seed. We planted (a/the) seeds. We watered them

with (a/an) hose. I can't wait to eat from (a/the) garden!

Vocabulary

Name It!

Grammar Rules Plural Nouns

- Add *s* to most nouns to show more than one.

  meal → meal<u>s</u>

- Add *es* to nouns that end with *ss, x, ch,* and *sh* to show more than one.

  lunch → lunch<u>es</u>

glass	sandwich	teacher	mother

meal		lunch

BEGIN

1. **Play with a partner.**
2. **Use a small object for a game piece.**
3. **Flip a coin.**

   = Move 1 space.

   = Move 2 spaces.
4. **Say the singular noun.**
5. **Write the plural form on another sheet of paper.**

END

6. **The first one to the END wins!**

park

box

brother	dish	class	bowl

Phonics

Letter and Sound Gg  _Gg_

Write the missing letter. Color each item named in the sentence.

1. girl	**2.** up	**3.** ift
4. at	**5.** ate	**6.** uitar
7. oat	**8.** ion	**9.** ink

Read It Together   Find the gate and the goat.

Phonics

Letter and Sound Dd

Write the missing letter. Color each item named in the sentence.

1. dog	2. oor	3. esk
4. ime	5. ink	6. uck
7. irl	8. oll	9. eer

Read It Together   Find the duck and the door.

Name _____ Date _____

Letter and Sound Vv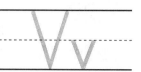

Write the missing letter. Color each item named in the sentence.

1.  _v_an	**2.**  _uck	**3.**  _eaf
4.  _ase	**5.**  _ing	**6.**  _og
7. _at	**8.** _est	**9.** _an

Read It Together   Find the vest and the vase.

PM1.40

Name _____ Date _____

Letter and Sound Rr

Write the missing letter. Color each item named in the sentence.

1. _r_ug	**2.** _en	**3.** _ap
4. _oad	**5.** _ing	**6.** _ake
7. _ish	**8.** _ope	**9.** _and

Read It Together   Find the rake and the rug.

For use with TE p. T31q   **PM1.41**   **Unit 1 | Family**

Name _____ Date _____

High Frequency Words

Trace each word two times and then write it.

get get get

help help help

of of of

put put put

we we we

work work work

For use with TE p. T33h

Unit 1 | Family

Cut out the pictures and the book. Fold the book on the solid lines. Paste a *g* picture on each page and write its name. Read the sentence and do what it says.

Read It Together

Put an X on the cat.

My G g Book

Name _____ Date _____

Cut out the pictures and the book. Fold the book on the solid lines. Paste a *d* picture on each page and write its name. Read the sentence and color what it names.

My D d Book

Read It Together

Find the dog.

PM1.44

Name _____ Date _____

Cut out the pictures and the book. Fold the book on the solid lines. Paste a *v* picture on each page and write its name. Read the sentence and color what it names.

Read It Together

My V v Book

Find the van.

Name _____ Date _____

Cut out the pictures and the book. Fold the book on the solid lines. Paste an *r* picture on each page and write its name. Read the sentence and do what it says.

My R r Book

Read It Together

Put an X on the fan.

High Frequency Word Cards

her	get
him	help
too	of
with	put
you	we
your	work

For use with TE p. T31i

PM1.47

Unit 1 | My Family

Name _____ Date _____

Identify Setting

Write the setting of a family story you know at the top of the left column. Write about the setting below. Draw a picture of the setting in the right column.

Setting: _____	Picture of the Place

Name _____ Date _____

Letter and Sound Oo

Write the missing letter. Put a dot by the item named.

1.  __ostrich__	**2.**  __ x__
3.  __tter__	**4.** 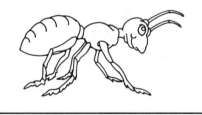 __nt__
5.  __ish__	**6.**  __live__

Read It Together   Put a big dot by the ox.

For use with TE p. T35e

A Big Help

Write a word from the box to complete each sentence.

High Frequency Words
get
help
of
put
we
work

_____

1. I _____ with Mom.

2. We _____ a ham.

3. We _____ the ham in a pan.

4. My dog can _____ , too.

5. My dog can do a lot _____ work!

Name _____ Date _____

Use Proper Nouns

1. **Point to a picture.**

2. **Use a common noun to name the place.**

3. **Then use a proper noun to name the place. Make up a name or use the name of a real place.**

4. **Say your sentences to your partner.**

Name _____ Date _____

Cut out the pictures and the book. Fold the book on the solid lines. Paste an *o* picture on each page and write its name. Read the sentence and do what it says.

Read It Together

Put an X on the cap.

My O o Book

Name _____   Date _____

Final -s

Circle the word that completes each sentence and write it.

hat   **hats**

_____

- - - - - - - - - - - - - -

1. Bob has lots of _____ .

has   **his**

_____

- - - - - - - - - - - - - -

2. Bob _____ a dog, too.

has   **is**

_____

- - - - - - - - - - - - - -

3. Rags _____ his dog.

get   **gets**

_____

- - - - - - - - - - - - - -

4. Bob _____ Rags a hat.

his   **is**

_____

- - - - - - - - - - - - - -

5. Rags likes _____ hat.

Grammar and Writing

Write Common and Proper Nouns

| state | dog | Shell Beach | brother | Miami | Ashley |

Look at each pair of sentences. Look at the <u>underlined word</u> in the first sentence. Draw a line to the common or proper noun that completes the second sentence.

1. This is my <u>sister</u>.

Her name is _____ .

brother

2. This is <u>James</u>.

He is my _____ .

Ashley

3. We live in a big <u>city</u>.

It is called _____ .

Miami

4. Miami is in <u>Florida</u>.

Our _____ is in the south.

state

5. We swim at the <u>beach</u>.

We often go to _____ .

dog

6. <u>Buddy</u> splashes in the waves with us. Buddy is our _____ .

Shell Beach

Vocabulary

Family Trip Bingo

1. Write one Key Word in each suitcase.

2. Listen to the clues. Place a marker on the Key Word.

3. Say "Bingo" when you have four markers in a row.

Setting Chart

Papá and Me

List the places that Papá and his son went. Then list words that tell what the places are like.

Places	What the Places are Like
• home	• fun
•	•
•	•
•	•

 Take turns with a partner. Use your setting chart to give information about the story.

Name _____ Date _____

Letter and Sound Bb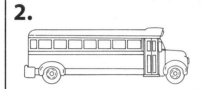

Write the missing letter. Color the item named in the sentence.

1.  __ <u>b</u>at	**2.**  __us	**3.**  __un
4.  __an	**5.**  __ed	**6.**  __an
7.  __ee	**8.**  __ird	**9.**  __oy

Read It Together   Find the bed.

Name _____ Date _____

Letter and Sound Ww

Write the missing letter. Color each item named in the sentence.

1. _____ w e b	2. _____ o p e	3. _____ a v e
4. _____ e l l	5. _____ e e	6. _____ i n g
7. _____ i g	8. _____ o o k	9. _____ a n

Read It Together   Find the wing and the well.

PM1.58

Name _____ Date _____

Letter and Sound Jj

 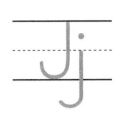

Write the missing letter. Put a dot on the item named.

1. jeans	**2.** acket	**3.** og
4. eer	**5.** et	**6.** eal
7. ion	**8.** ar	**9.** ips

Read It Together   Put a dot on the jet.

Phonics

Letter and Sound Zz  _Zz_

Write the missing letter. Color each item named in the sentence.

1.

_t_ub

2.

_ipper

3.

_ero

4.

_ase

5.

_oo

6.

_ock

Read It Together Find the zoo and the zipper.

Name _____   Date _____

Find Proper Nouns

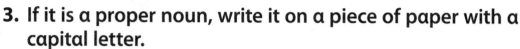

1. Take turns with a partner.

2. Read the word in the box.

3. If it is a proper noun, write it on a piece of paper with a capital letter.

4. If it is a common noun, don't write anything.

5. Color all the boxes with a proper noun to get Fluffy to the vet.

fluffy	nebraska	monday
home	trip	amy
idea	carlos	june
oak street	friday	share
october	group	visit
wisconsin	sunday	doctor dan

Handwriting

High Frequency Words

Trace each word two times and then write it.

day day day

from from from

good good good

she she she

us us us

very very very

Name _____ Date _____

Cut out the pictures and the book. Fold the book on the solid lines. Paste a *b* picture on each page and write its name. Read the sentence and color what it names.

My B b Book

Read It Together

Find the bat.

Name _____ Date _____

Cut out the pictures and the book. Fold the book on the solid lines. Paste a *w* picture on each page and write its name. Read the sentence and color what it names.

Read It Together

Find the wave.

My W w Book

Name _____ Date _____

Cut out the pictures and the book. Fold the book on the solid lines. Paste a *j* picture on each page and write its name. Read the sentence and do what it says.

Read It Together

Put an X on the hat.

My J j Book

Cut out the pictures and the book. Fold the book on the solid lines. Paste a *z* picture on each page and write its name. Read the sentence and do what it says.

Read It Together

My Z z Book

Put an X on the wig.

High Frequency Word Cards

get	day
help	from
of	good
put	she
we	us
work	very

Name _____ Date _____

Compare Genres

Compare a story and a postcard.

Realistic Fiction	Postcard
is a made up story that seems real	is a message from a real person

 Tell a partner how a story and a postcard are different.

Letter and Sound Ee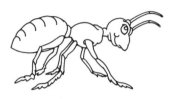

Write the missing letter. Color each item named in the sentence.

1.

___e___gg

2.

___nt

3.

___levator

4.

___lbow

5.

___nvelope

6.

___orse

Read It Together   Find the egg and the elbow.

   PM1.69

Name _____ Date _____

Zip Can Jog

Write a word from the box to complete each sentence.

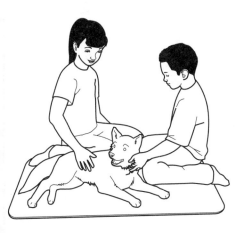

High Frequency Words
day
from
good
she
us
very

1. Zip is a _____ dog.

2. Zip can jog _____ the bed to the mat.

3. Zip can get a big pat from _____ .

4. _____ can jog from the mat to the bed.

5. Zip has a very good _____ !

Cut out the pictures and the book. Fold the book on the solid lines. Paste an *e* picture on each page and write its name. Read the sentence and do what it says.

Read It Together

Put an E on the leg.

My E e Book

Grammar and Writing

Proper Nouns and Dates

Look at each sentence. Circle the correct ending.

seattle.

1. Jen lives in

 Seattle.

Tim.

2. She lives with her mom and her brother

tim.

Texas.

3. Jen's family took a trip to

texas.

July 18 2013.

4. They left on

July 18, 2013.

monday.

5. They came home the next

Monday.

july!

6. Jen learned that Texas can be very hot in

July!

Name _____ Date _____

Name Game

Grammar Rules Proper Nouns

Start a proper noun
with a capital letter. $\longrightarrow$ My dog <u>Mac</u> is the
best dog in the world.

1. **Play with a partner.**
2. **Spin the spinner.**
3. **Name a proper noun. Write the proper noun on a piece of paper.**

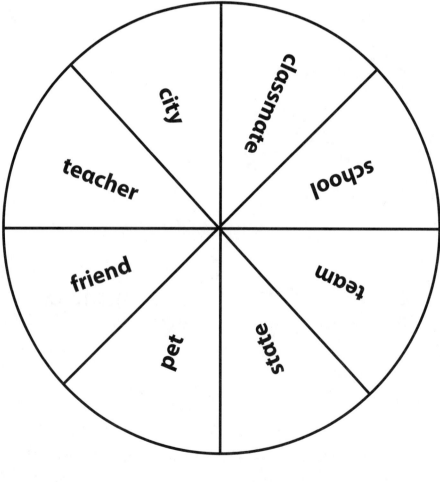

Make a Spinner

1. Put a paper clip in the center of the circle.

2. Hold one end of the paper clip with a pencil.

3. Spin the paper clip around the pencil.

Name _____ Date _____

Idea Web

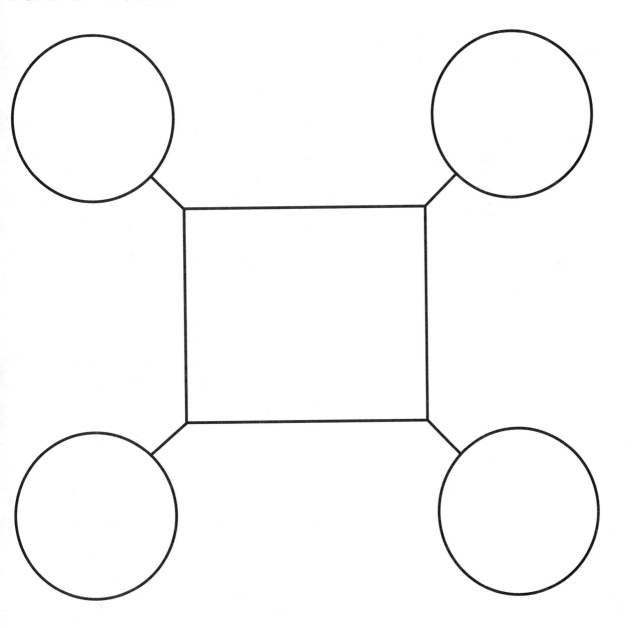

Word Choice Checklist

✓ Did you pick strong words?

✓ Do your words go with your pictures?

✓ Do your words grab your reader's attention?

PM1.74

Letter and Sound Yy

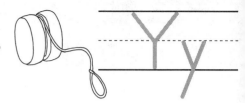

Name what is in each picture.
Write the missing letter.

1.

y̶arn

2.

olk

3.

amp

4.

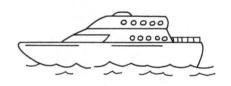

acht

5.

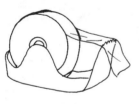

ape

6.

ut

Read It Together   Can you find the nut? Yes, I can!

© National Geographic Learning, a part of Cengage Learning, Inc.
For use with TE p. T67c

Unit 2 | Shoot for the Sun

Name _____   Date _____

Letter and Sound Qq

Name what is in each picture. Write the missing letter.

1.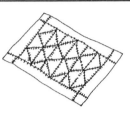

quilt

2.

ave

3.

ig

4.

uarter

5.

uart

6.

ing

Read It Together   Can I quit? Yes, you can.

PM2.2   Unit 2 | Shoot for the Sun

Name _____   Date _____

Letter and Sound Xx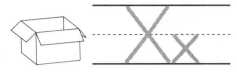

Cut out and name the picture cards. Trace the words. Put in the box the cards with names that end like *box*.

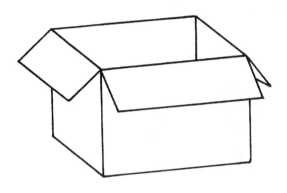

- ✂ - - - - - - - -

six	top	fox	tub
rug	ax	ox	pen

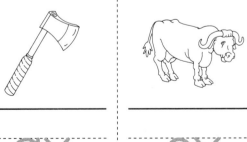

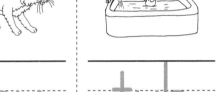

Read It Together   What is in your box?

For use with TE p. T67c   **PM2.3**   Unit 2 | Shoot for the Sun

Name _____ Date _____

Letter and Sound Kk

Name what is in each picture. Write the missing letter.

1. k ey	**2.** obe	**3.** it
4. oll	**5.** ing	**6.** ox
7. ite	**8.** itten	**9.** ake

Read It Together   Find the kit and the fox.

Name _____ Date _____

List Facts

Use the checklist. Decide if something is living or nonliving.

Living Things Checklist	
can eat	☐
can drink	☐
is healthy	☐
can think	☐

Phonics

Words with 's

Circle the word that completes each sentence.
Write the word on the line. Read the sentences.

Sam   **Sam's**
_____

----

1. What is in _____ box?

Jen   **Jen's**
_____

----

2. Mom finds _____ cap in the box.

Dad   **Dad's**
_____

----

3. _____ hat is in the box, too.

Quin   **Quin's**
_____

----

4. _____ can not find his cat in the box.

Bev   **Bev's**
_____

----

5. The cat naps on _____ mat.

For use with TE p. T70d   **PM2.6**   **Unit 2** | Shoot for the Sun

Name _____ Date _____

High Frequency Words

Trace each word two times and then write it.

for for for

grow grow grow

keep keep keep

look look look

or or or

when when when

Name _____ Date _____

Cut out the pictures and the book. Fold the book on the solid lines. Paste a y picture on each page and write its name. Read the sentence and color what it names.

Read It Together

Find the yam.

My Y y Book

PM2.8

Cut out the pictures and the book. Fold the book on the solid lines.
Paste a *q* picture on each page and write its name.

Read It Together

Is this a Q?
Yes, it is a big Q!

Q

My Q q Book

Name _____ Date _____

Cut out the pictures and the book. Fold the book on the solid lines. Paste an *x* picture on each page and write its name. Draw a picture in the box that answers the question.

Read It Together

My X x Book

What do you have in a box?

_____

- - - - - - - - - - -

_____

_____

- - - - - - - - - - -

_____

_____

- - - - - - - - - - -

_____

PM2.10

Name _____ Date _____

Cut out the pictures and the book. Fold the book on the solid lines. Paste a *k* picture on each page and write its name. Read the sentence and color what it names.

My K k Book

Read It Together

Find the kid.

High Frequency Word Cards

find	for
has	grow
have	keep
his	look
mother	or
too	when

Phonics

Letter and Sound Uu

Name what is in each picture. Write the missing letter.

1.  umpire	**2.**  pple
3.  ouse	**4.** nderwear
5.  ncle	**6.**  eal

Read It Together   Can a cub tug a tub in the mud?

Name _____ Date _____

It Can Grow!

Look at the pictures. Write a word from the box to complete each sentence.

High Frequency **Words**
for
grow
keep
look
or
when

_____

1. _____ can Jen get a pup?

_____

2. This little pup is a good pup _____ Jen.

_____

3. Jen can _____ this little pup!

_____

4. Look at the little pup _____ !

_____

5. Is it a little pup _____ a big dog?

Grammar: Adjectives

Use Determiners

Cut out the words on the petals. Glue five petals around each center.
Then make sentences with the word in the center and each petal.

(that)   (those)

(these)   (this)

hat	gloves	garden	hose
plant	shoes	shirt	pants
socks	kittens	dog	rabbit
glasses	pen	doors	window

Name _____ Date _____

Cut out the pictures and the book. Fold the book on the solid lines. Paste a *u* picture on each page and write its name. Read the question and draw a picture.

Read It Together

Can a cub sit in the sun?

My U u Book

Grammar & Writing

Write Adjectives

Read the story. Then choose a word from the box that goes with the sentence. Write it on the line.

this	that	these	those	fat	green

Amy looked at the garden. "What is _____*that*_____

thing over by the fence?" she asked her mom. On the

_____

ground she saw a _____ green worm. Her

mom picked it up. She said, "_____ caterpillar

is fat. It likes to eat _____ plant stems. Her

mom pointed to the last row of tomatoes. "I found

_____

many caterpillars on _____ plants!" Then she

looked down at the bean plants next to her feet. "I don't

think the caterpillars like to eat _____ beans,"

she said.

Unit 2 | Shoot for the Sun

Vocabulary

Rivet

1. Write the first letter of each word.

2. Have a partner try to guess the word.

3. Fill in letters one at a time until your partner guesses the word.

1. ___ ___ ___ ___ ___ ___ ___ ___

2. ___ ___ ___ ___

3. ___ ___ ___ ___ ___ ___ ___

4. ___ ___ ___ ___ ___ ___ ___

5. ___ ___ ___ ___ ___

6. ___ ___ ___ ___ ___ ___ ___ ___

7. ___ ___ ___ ___ ___

8. ___ ___ ___ ___ ___ ___

9. ___ ___ ___ ___

10. ___ ___ ___ ___ ___ ___ ___ ___ ___

11. ___ ___ ___ ___ ___ ___ ___ ___ ___

 Take turns with a partner. Choose a word. Say it in a sentence.

Name _____   Date _____

Are You Living?

**Add facts you learned about living things to the checklist.
Place checks in the boxes.**

Living Things Checklist	
can eat	☐
can drink	☐
is healthy	☐
can think	☐
	☐
	☐
	☐
	☐

**Take turns with a partner. Tell a fact that you learned about
living things in "Are You Living?"**

Name _____ Date _____

Phonics

Double Consonants

we**ll**

Name what is in each picture. Draw a line from the first letter to the rest of the word. Write the word and read it.

1.	2.	3.
og	uzz	ill
d ······· oll	b oll	m itt
do**ll**	_____	_____

3.	5.	6.
oss	ell	uff
t iff	b ut	h ill
_____	_____	_____

Read It Together   What can you toss to a pal with a mitt?

Name _____ Date _____

Phonics

Double Consonants

Cut along the dotted lines. Write *t, b, l, m* in each box of one pull strip and *b, f, s, y* in each box of the other. Put the strips through the slits with the arrows pointing up. Read the words you make.

 to<u>ss</u>

 be<u>ll</u>

oss

ell

For use with TE p. T91b
PM2.21

Name _____ Date _____

Blend Words

Name what is in each picture. Circle the word that goes with the picture.

1.  bed (bell)	**2.**  add egg	**3.**  us up
4.  an man	**5.** 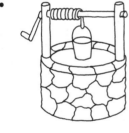 wax well	**6.** 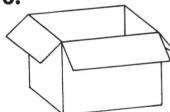 box ox
7.  hill hat	**8.**  is up	**9.**  ill if

Read It Together Can you put a bell in a box?

PM2.22

Handwriting

High Frequency Words

Trace each word two times and then write it.

body body body

how how how

out out out

start start start

they they they

use use use

Word Sort: Double Final Consonants

egg	bill	doll	cuff
pass	puff	buzz	hiss
tell	odd	fuzz	fill
off	lass	mess	dull
fell	muss	will	huff
well	add	mill	jazz
yell	kiss	fizz	pill

High Frequency Word Cards

do	body
then	how
what	out
with	start
you	they
your	use

T-Chart

Compare Genres

Compare a song and a diagram.

Song	Diagram
	has numbered steps

 Work with a partner. Take turns asking about a song and a diagram.

Phonics

Words with <u>ck</u>, <u>ng</u>

duck

sing

Name what is in each picture. Circle the word that goes with each picture.

1. will (wing) wig	**2.** taps tan tack
3. sock sobs song	**4.** rip ring rock
5. kill kick king	**6.** loss lock long

Read It Together   A king has a ring. What has a wing?

Name _____ Date _____

Tug, Tug, Tug

**Look at the picture.
Write a word from the box
to complete each sentence.**

High Frequency **Words**
body
how
out
start
they
use

1. The dog can not get _____ !

2. His _____ is too big.

3. _____ will the dog get out?

4. Tom and Tim _____ to help.

5. They _____ rags and tug, tug, tug!

Name _____ Date _____

Use Shades of Meaning

Read the adjective below each box. Then draw a picture in the box to show something that the adjective may describe. Here are some ideas you can draw.

apples	bugs	dogs	flowers	hats	shoes	trees	trucks

small	**tiny**	**itsy-bitsy**
big	**huge**	**enormous**

Phonics

Words with <u>ck</u>, <u>ng</u>

Cut along the dotted lines. Write *d, l, r, s* in each box of one pull strip and *k, r, s, w* in each box of the other. Put the strips through the slits with the arrows pointing up. Read the words you make.

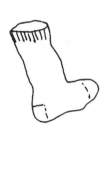 sock

 wing

 ock

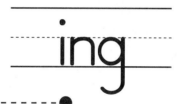 ing

Grammar & Writing

Write More Adjectives

Read the story. Then choose a word from the box that goes with the sentence. Write it on the line.

green	heavy	round	tiny

Jared and Paul planted a bag of seeds. "Wow,"

said Paul, "these seeds are so ___tiny___, I can

hardly see them." For a week, nothing happened. The

boys kept watering the seeds. The watering can was

_____

_____ and hard to lift. After a few weeks,

they saw little _____ leaves coming out of the

soil. By the end of the month, they were eating delicious

_____ radishes.

Grammar: Adjectives

Draw It!

Grammar Rules Adjectives

1. Adjectives describe how something looks.

2. Some adjectives tell about color, size, or shape.

The green plant is tall.

Read each sentence. Draw a line under each adjective. Then use the sentences to draw a picture on a separate piece on paper.

1. The park has green grass and yellow flowers.

2. Children play with a big, red ball.

3. A small, brown bird flies above.

4. A boy sees a blue house with square windows.

5. A tall man sells round balloons in many colors and sizes.

💬 **Take turns with a partner. Show your picture and describe it.**

Name _____ Date _____

Blends fl, pl, sl

flag

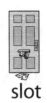
plug

slot

Name what is in each picture. Circle the word that goes with each picture.

1.

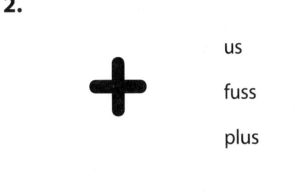

(flag)

bag

wag

2.

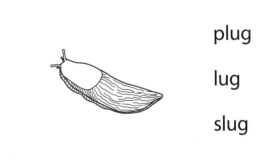

us

fuss

plus

3.

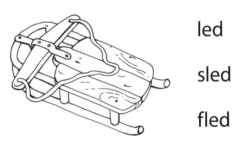

led

sled

fled

4.

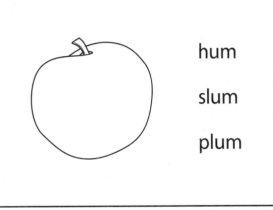

hum

slum

plum

5.

plug

lug

slug

6.

flock

lock

sock

Read It Together   Find a flag and a slug.

For use with TE p. T93q   **PM2.33**   **Unit 2** | Shoot for the Sun

Name _____ Date _____

Identify Plot

Retell a story you know to a partner. Fill out the chart.

Title: _____

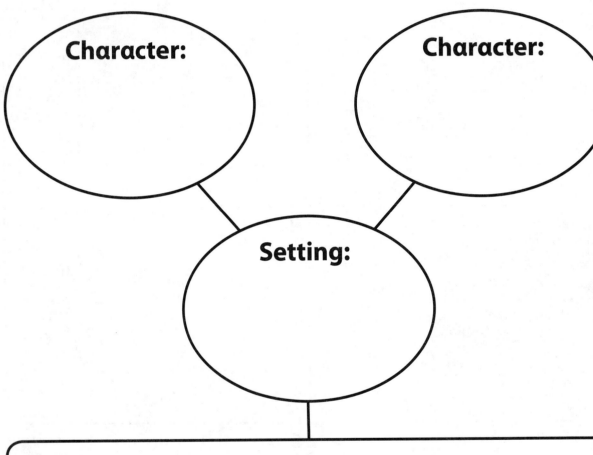

Plot:

Phonics

Blends f̲l̲, p̲l̲, s̲l̲

Name what is in each picture. Draw a line from the blends on the left to the rest of the word. Write the word and read it.

1.

ed

sl ············· ot

slot

2.

um

pl

ug

3.

at

fl

ag

4.

us

pl

uck

5.

ock

fl

ick

6.

id

sl

ug

Read It Together   Sid and Sam slid on the sled.

Phonics

Blend words

Circle the word that names each picture. Read the word.

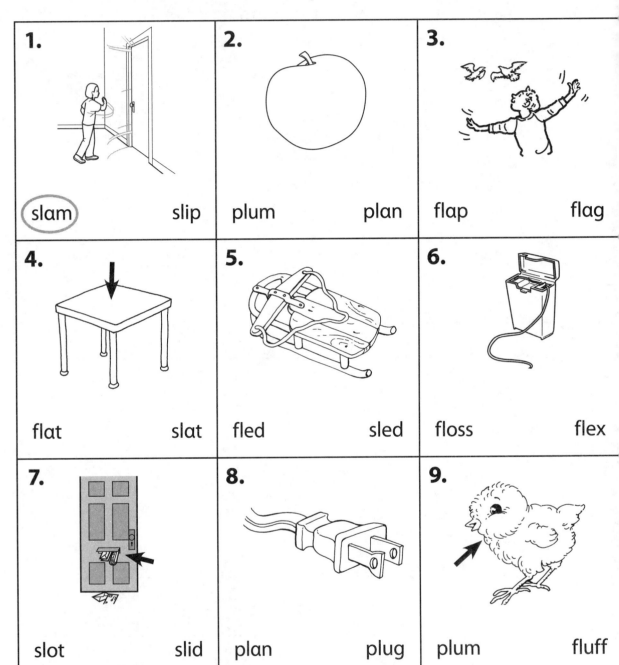

1. (slam) slip	**2.** plum plan	**3.** flap flag
4. flat slat	**5.** fled sled	**6.** floss flex
7. slot slid	**8.** plan plug	**9.** plum fluff

Read It Together   It is flat. Can it flap?

Name _____   Date _____

High Frequency Words

Trace each word two times and then write it.

does does does

eat eat eat

live live live

no no no

see see see

why why why

Word Cards: *fl, pl, sl*

flag	plug	sled	flock
fling	flip	flat	slit
flap	plan	plum	slip
plus	flick	slick	slam
slap	slop	flop	fled
pluck	slim	fluff	slung
sling	plop	slug	fleck

High Frequency Word Cards

get

does

help

eat

of

live

put

no

we

see

work

why

For use with TE p. T93i

PM2.39

Unit 2 | Shoot for the Sun

Name _____ Date _____

Blends cl, gl, bl

 class
 glob
 block

Circle the word that names each picture. Read the word.

1. 	cap flap (clap)
2.	black flack back
3. 	glad lad clad
4. 	lock clock flock
5. 	gas class glass
6. 	click block flick

Read It Together Do you clap when you are glad?

PM2.40 Unit 2 | Shoot for the Sun

Name _____ Date _____

What Is It?

Look at the picture. Write a word from the box to complete each sentence.

High Frequency Words
does
eat
live
no
see
why

_____

1. _____ it start in an egg? Yes!

2. Do you _____ it peck? Yes!

3. Yum! Will it _____ a bug? Yes!

4. Can it live in your bed? _____ , it can not!

5. _____ not? It is a hen!

PM2.41

Word Cards: Adjectives

some	a lot	much	a little
many	a few	three	six
hat	glove	garden	water
shovel	bread	dirt	air
plant	shoe	shirt	seed
wind	kitten	dog	rain
glasses	pen	food	furniture
snow	plate	apple	banana

Phonics

Blends cl, gl, bl

**Draw a line from the blend on the left to the rest of the word.
Write the word and read it.**

1. cl ·········· ip iff _clip_	**2.** gl ad um	**3.** gl ob ad
4. bl ot ess	**5.** cl am ub	**6.** bl ab uff

Read It Together   Do you use black blocks and clips in class?

Phonics

Short <u>a</u>, <u>i</u>

Circle the word that completes each sentence.
Write the word on the line. Read the sentences.

quick	quack

1. A duck likes to _____ .

flap	slip

2. A duck likes to _____ its wings, too.

3. What does Cliff like to do?

sing	sang

Cliff likes to _____ .

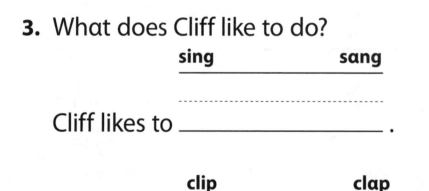

clip	clap

4. Pam likes to _____ for Cliff.

5. What does a dog like to do?

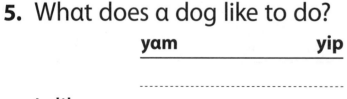

yam	yip

It likes to _____ and yap!

Name _____ Date _____

Write Indefinite Adjectives

Read the letter. Then choose a word from the box that goes with each sentence.

a few	a little	many	much	some

Hi Uncle Ray,

Did you hear that we are planting a garden this year?

Last year, some friends gave us only _____ a few _____

tomatoes, but that was not enough for us. It was so

_____

_____ work to plant everything. If we get

_____

_____ rain, I'm sure our plants will grow. I

_____

hope we get _____ tomatoes this year. I love

_____

to eat them with _____ salt.

> Love,
> Amber

**Vocabulary**

Around the World

1. The traveler stands behind a challenger.

2. Listen to the clue. Find the Key Word and say it.

3. The first to answer correctly travels to the next student on the right. The first traveler to go all around the circle wins.

KEY WORDS

seed	bud	petal	flower	leaf

CLUES

- a part of a plant that is the start of a flower

- the flat, green part of a plant

- the flat part of a flower

- a part of a plant that is small and grows into a new plant

- a part of a plant that has many petals

Name _____ Date _____

The Daisy

Complete the chart. Describe what happens to the little seed in "The Daisy."

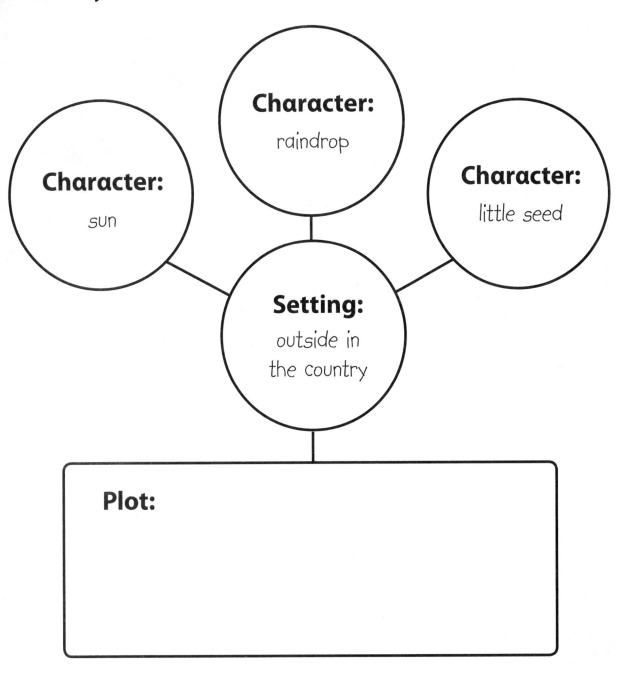

Character:
raindrop

Character:
sun

Character:
little seed

Setting:
outside in
the country

Plot:

 Take turns with a partner. Use your chart to describe what happens to the little seed.

Name _____ Date _____

Blends <u>fr</u>, <u>gr</u>, <u>tr</u>

 <u>fr</u>og   <u>gr</u>ass   <u>tr</u>uck

Circle the word that goes with each picture. Read the word.

1. 	fog frog flag	**2.** 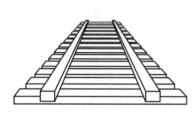	track tuck pluck
3. 	trot frizz class	**4.** 	tap trap flap
5. 	gas glass grass	**6.** 	grub rub club

Read It Together   We can see a grub in the grass.

Unit 2 | Shoot for the Sun

Name _____ Date _____

Blends <u>fr</u>, <u>gr</u>, <u>tr</u>

Draw a line from the blend on the left to the rest of the word.
Write the word and read it.

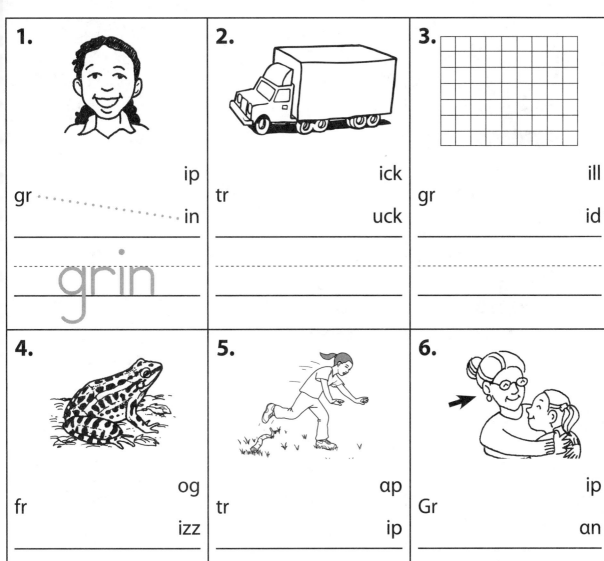

1.

gr .... ip
.... in

grin

2.

tr   ick
   uck

3.

gr   ill
   id

4.

fr   og
   izz

5.

tr   ap
   ip

6.

Gr   ip
   an

Read It Together Tran trots to the truck.

© National Geographic Learning, a part of Cengage Learning, Inc.
For use with TE p. T125a

PM2.49

Unit 2 | Shoot for the Sun

Blend words

Circle the word that goes with each picture. Read the word.

1. club (clam)	**2.** slug plug	**3.** clock click
4. plus plan	**5.** clog frog	**6.** plot glob
7. block black	**8.** grin grip	**9.** flag flat

Read It Together   The black clock ticks and tocks.

Name _____ Date _____

High Frequency Words

Trace each word two times and then write it.

all all all

are are are

by by by

first first first

more more more

there there there

Word Cards: *fr, gr, tr, br, cr, dr*

frog	grass	truck	drop
frill	dress	drank	crop
grab	grow	grin	grunt
drill	crab	trim	trap
frizz	grub	gruff	drip
trip	grid	brim	brink
grip	crib	cram	Fred

High Frequency Word Cards

day	all
from	are
good	by
she	first
us	more
very	there

Name _____ Date _____

Compare Genres

Compare a fairy tale and a project notebook.

Fairy Tale	Project Notebook
is a fantasy	is nonfiction

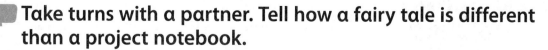 **Take turns with a partner. Tell how a fairy tale is different than a project notebook.**

Name _____ Date _____

Blends <u>br</u>, <u>cr</u>, <u>dr</u>

brick

crab

drum

Circle the word that goes with each picture. Read the word.

1.		2.	
	slim		rib
	grim		crib
	(brim)		drill

3.		4.	
	dress		grip
	press		drop
	brass		crop

5.		6.	
	tricks		drip
	bricks		grip
	clicks		trip

Read It Together   Grab that brick, and do not drop it.

For use with TE p. T126c   **PM2.55**   Unit 2 | Shoot for the Sun

Name _____ Date _____

Yum!

Look at the pictures. Write a word from the box to complete each sentence.

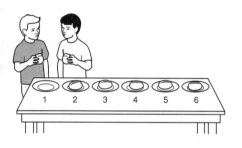
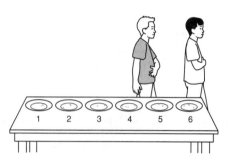

High Frequency Words
all
are
by
first
more
there

_____
\- -

1. There _____ six buns.

_____
\- -

2. Matt and Bill pass _____ the buns.

_____
\- -

3. They eat the _____ bun.

_____
\- -

4. Then they eat _____ the buns!

_____
\- -

5. There are no _____ buns.

Grammar: Adjectives

Use Indefinite Adjectives

Use a number cube with six numbers to play the game. Roll the cube and find your number on the chart.

Chart

1	2	3	4	5	6
some	a few	a little	many	much	a lot

Say a sentence using the word that matches your number. If all of the players agree that your sentence is correct, mark it off on the score sheet.

Score Sheet

Player 1 _____ Player 2 _____ Player 3 _____

1		1		1	
2		2		2	
3		3		3	
4		4		4	
5		5		5	
6		6		6	

Name _____   Date _____

Blends <u>br</u>, <u>cr</u>, <u>dr</u>

**Draw a line from the blend on the left to the rest of the word.
Write the word and read it.**

1.	2.	3.
X		
ops	ag	ib
cr · · · · · · · · · oss	dr ill	cr ack
cross		

4.	5.	6.
op	icks	ing
dr ess	br ag	br im

Phonics

Short <u>o</u>, <u>e</u>, <u>u</u>

Circle the word that completes each sentence. Write the word on the line. Read the sentences.

red   **rod**
_____

1. Fred has a little _____ hen.

clocks   **clucks**
_____

2. Fred's hen _____ a lot.

pecks   **pucks**
_____

3. It _____ in the mud, too.

begs   **bugs**
_____

4. The hen finds _____ to eat. Yum!

5. The hen does not like to eat

crops   **cribs**
_____

Fred's _____ !

Name _____ Date _____

Write Indefinite Adjectives

Read the play. Then choose a word from the box that goes with each sentence.

| some | a little | many | how many | how much |

Kala is helping her father work in the family garden.

Father: Kala, please pour ___*a little*___ water on that row of beans. Not too much.

Kala: _____ plants look yellow and dry.

_____ rain do we need?

Father: I think three or four days of rain will really help our plants.

Kala: _____ hours have we been working in the sun?

Father: Maybe it's time to stop. Let's go get

_____ ice cream.

Grammar: Adjectives

At School

Grammar Rules Adjectives

1. Some adjectives tell how many there are of something.

   I ate <u>three</u> pears.

2. Some adjectives tell how much there is of something.

   I need <u>some</u> water.

Complete the sentences below. Use words from the box.

much	some	five	many	ten

1. There are __many__ books in the library.

2. There are _____ soccer balls in the gym.

3. There is _____ food in the cafeteria.

4. There is not _____ milk in the cafeteria.

5. There are _____ pencils on the desk.

Write two sentences about your school. Use adjectives.
Read them to a partner.

Name _____ Date _____

Steps in a Process Diagram

Materials: _____

_____

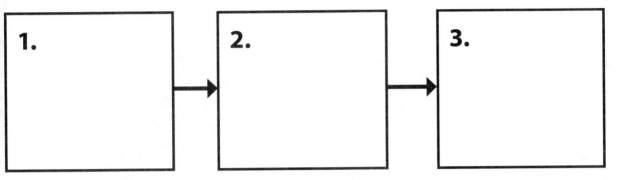

Organization Checklist

✓ Did you list what you need?

✓ Did you write what to do?

✓ Did you list the steps in order?

✓ Did you number the steps?

Blends with s̲

 spot   **swing**   **sling**

Circle the word that names each picture. Read and answer the question. Act out each action.

1.
slim
skim
(swim)

2.
(spin)
grin
skin

3.
sped
(sled)
slug

4.
(steps)
snaps
scabs

5.
snip
slip
(skip)

6.
spell
(smell)
swell

Read It Together Can you skip, swim, spin, and sled?

Name _____ Date _____

Categorize Needs and Wants

List what you need and what you want in the T-chart below.

Need	Want
• peas	• toy car
• fish	• ball
•	•
•	•
•	•

Phonics

Blends with s

Draw a line from the first two letters to the rest of the word. Write the word and read it. Read the sentence.

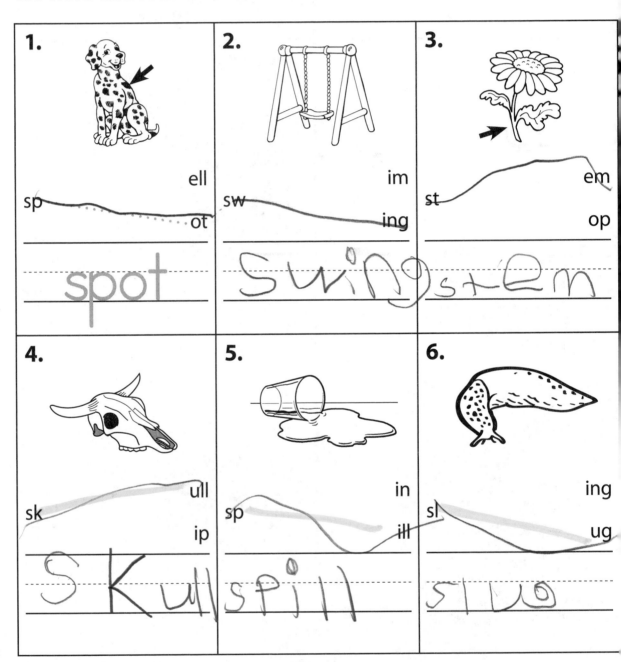

1.
ell
sp
ot

spot

2.
im
sw
ing

swing

3.
em
st
op

stem

4.
ull
sk
ip

Skull

5.
in
sp
ill

spill

6.
ing
sl
ug

slug

Read It Together   Stan sees a slug on the swing.

Name _____ Date _____

High Frequency Words

Trace each word two times and then write it.

go go go

great great great

one one one

saw saw saw

want want want

would would would

Word Cards: Words with *s* Blends

stack	snack	swim	sled
smack	spot	skill	swamp
step	smell	sling	skip
spill	swell	skid	stem
spend	skin	slam	smart
swing	slid	spin	sniff
snap	snug	stuck	small

High Frequency Word Cards

for	go
grow	great
keep	one
look	saw
or	want
when	would

For use with TE p. T131k   **PM3.6**   **Unit 3** | To Your Front Door

Name ___Max___ Date _____

Phonics

Triple Blends with s

string

Circle the word that names the picture. Read the sentence.

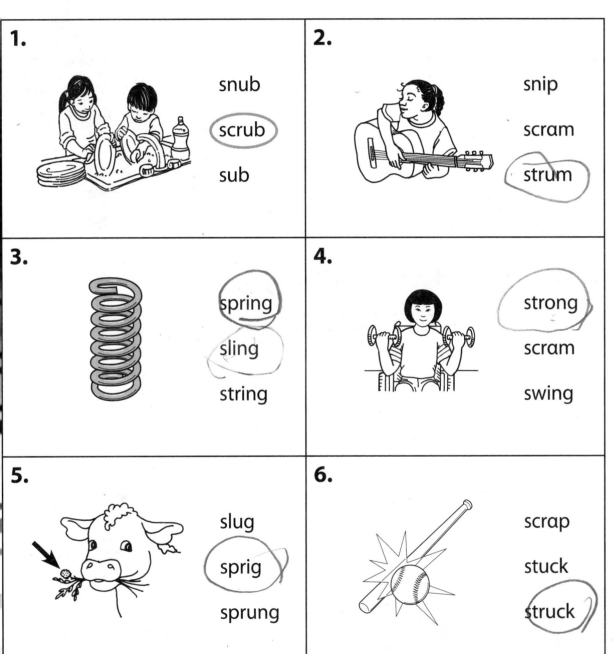

1.
snub
(scrub)
sub

2.
snip
scram
(strum)

3.
(spring)
sling
string

4.
(strong)
scram
swing

5.
slug
(sprig)
sprung

6.
scrap
stuck
(struck)

Read It Together   The strong cat springs to get the string.

Name _____ Date _____

The Sled

Look at the picture. Write a word from the box to complete each sentence.

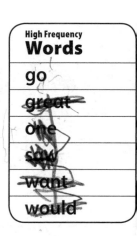

High Frequency **Words**
go
~~great~~
~~one~~
~~saw~~
~~want~~
would

1. What did I see? I _saw_ sleds on a hill.

2. My pal slid on _one_ sled.

3. I _want_ to get a sled, too.

4. I _would_ get on it and go, go, go!

5. I would have _great_ fun on my sled!

Name _____ Date _____

Use Action Verbs

1. Toss two markers on the game board. Toss one marker on the left side and one marker on the right side.

2. Say the word or words on the left. Name the action in the picture on the right.

3. Use the words in a sentence.

4. Play until each player has said five sentences.

He	
She	
The boy	
The Girl	
The man	
The woman	
The apple	
It	

For use with TE p. T131n

Triple Blends with <u>s</u>

Name the picture. Draw a line from the first three letters to the rest of the word. Write the word and read it. Read and act out the sentences.

1.	2.	3.
scr ···········aps / ams	str ess / ing	spr ing / ig
scraps		
4.	5.	6.
str ap / ut	scr uff / ub	spr ung / ig

Read It Together   Spring up. Scrub up. Strut off.

Phonics

Endings -s, -ing

Take one card. Find the person with a card that has the same word on it, even if that word has a different ending. Say the words and use them in a sentence.

kick	**kicks**
quack	**quacks**
smell	**smells**
swing	**swinging**
sniff	**sniffing**
duck	**ducking**

Name _____ Date _____

Write Present Tense Verbs

Subject	Action Verb
I	eat
We	shop
You	buy
They	sell
The girls	walk
He	eats
She	sells
It	walks
The boy	buys
The tree	grows

Read each sentence. Circle the correct verb. Write the verb.

1. We _____ through the market.
   walk
   walks

2. The man _____ fruit.
   sell
   sells

3. Kate _____ an orange.
   buy
   buys

4. Tom and I _____ grapes.
   buy
   buys

5. Kate _____ her orange.
   eat
   eats

6. We _____ our grapes.
   eat
   eats

7. They _____ fast.
   disappear
   disappears

Vocabulary

Rivet

1. Write the first letter of each word.

2. Try to guess the word.

3. Fill in the other letters of the word.

1. ____ ____ ____ ____ ____

2. ____ ____ ____ ____ ____

3. ____ ____ ____ ____ ____

4. ____ ____ ____ ____ ____

5. ____ ____ ____

6. ____ ____ ____ ____ ____ ____ ____ ____

7. ____ ____ ____ ____ ____

8. ____ ____ ____

9. ____ ____ ____ ____

10. ____ ____ ____ ____

 Take turns with a partner. Choose a word. Say it in a sentence.

Name _____ Date _____

Markets

List types of markets that you read about. List what each market sells in the What It Sells column.

Type of Market	What It Sells
• fruit market	• bananas, pears, grapes
•	•
•	•
•	•

 Take turns with a partner. Tell what you learned about markets. Use your T-chart.

Name _____ Date _____

Final <u>nd</u>, <u>nk</u>, <u>nt</u>

ha<u>nd</u>   si<u>nk</u>   te<u>nt</u>

Circle the word that names the picture. Read and answer the question.

1. 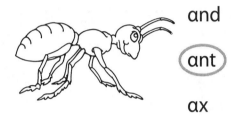 and (ant) ax	**2.**  skunk skin skull
3.  plant plank plan	**4.**  pick pink pond
5.  bend bell bed	**6.**  back bank band

Read It Together   Does Hank see a skunk or an ant by the pond?

PM3.15

Name _____ Date _____

Final <u>nd</u>, <u>nk</u>, <u>nt</u>

Write the letters to complete the word. Read and answer the question.

1.

sink

2.

te

3.

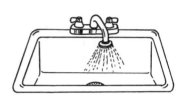

ha

4.

tru

5.

pla

6.

po

Read It Together   Can you put a hand or a trunk in the sink?

PM3.16

Name _____ Date _____

High Frequency Words

Trace each word two times and then write it.

give give give

he he he

know know know

said said said

watch watch watch

who who who

Word Cards: Final Blends -nd, -nk, -nt, -st, -mp, -ft, -sk, -lt

hand	sink	tent	lamp
lift	honk	tank	best
mint	ask	cost	send
went	felt	gift	wilt
raft	pond	skunk	stamp
hint	melt	fast	stand
romp	whisk	mask	theft

High Frequency Word Cards

body	give
how	he
out	know
start	said
they	watch
use	who

For use with TE p. T155g　　　　　**PM3.19**　　　　　**Unit 3** | To Your Front Door

Name _____ Date _____

Compare Authors' Purpose

Compare the authors' purposes in the social studies and online articles.

	Markets	Flower Power
Topic	markets around the world	
Author's Purpose		

 Tell a partner how the authors' purposes in the social studies and online articles are alike and different.

Name _____ Date _____

More Final Blends

nest lamp gift desk belt

Circle the word that names the picture. Read and answer the question.

1.		2.	
milk fruit eggs	lick lift (list)		ramp raft rat
3.		**4.**	
	mat mast mask		quilt quick quack
5.		**6.**	
	vend vent vest	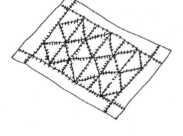	cap camp cast

Read It Together Do you want a mask, a vest, or a belt for a gift?

Name _____ Date _____

The Raft

Look at the picture. Write a word from the box to complete
each sentence. Read the sentences.

High Frequency **Words**
give
he
know
said
watch
who

_____

1. Dad _____ that he wants a raft.

_____

2. We _____ him one for a gift!

_____

3. Do you _____ if we can go on the raft
with Dad?

_____

4. Dad asks _____ wants to go with him.

5. Tess and I go. Mom and Frank sit on the bank

_____

and _____ .

Name _____ Date _____

Talk About Routines

Grammar Rules Routines

A routine word like <u>always</u>, <u>usually</u>, <u>sometimes</u>, or <u>never</u> tells how often someone does something.

The boy <u>sometimes</u> sings in the morning.

1. **Play with a partner.**

2. **Spin the spinner.**

3. **Tell about the person in the picture. Use a routine word and the present tense.**

Make a Spinner

1. Put a paper clip ⌐⊃ in the center of the circle.

2. Hold one end of the paper clip with a pencil.

3. Spin the paper clip around the pencil.

More Final Blends

Write the letters to complete the words. Read and act out the sentences.

1.

me|t

2.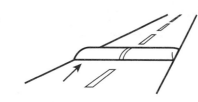

bu____

3.

re____

4.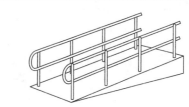

ra____

5.

ju____

6.

fa____

Read It Together   Jump and run fast. Then rest!

Name _____ Date _____

Phonics

Ending -<u>ed</u>

Read the word. Add -*ed* and write the new word on the line. Read the sentence.

sprint
_____

- - - - - - - - - - - - - - - - - - - -

1. Pam _____ .

pass
_____

- - - - - - - - - - - - - - - - - - - -

2. She _____ it.

kick
_____

- - - - - - - - - - - - - - - - - - - -

3. Jess _____ .

jump
_____

- - - - - - - - - - - - - - - - - - - -

4. Hank _____ .

block
_____

- - - - - - - - - - - - - - - - - - - -

5. Hank _____ it.

Name _____ Date _____

Write the Present Tense

1. Read each word in the word box.

2. Read each sentence. Write the correct word on the line in each sentence.

3. Use each word only once.

like	tell	read
washes	eats	mix

1. Sometimes, I ____ mix ____ pancakes for breakfast.

2. My sister _____ cereal every morning.

3. My dogs _____ a treat after their morning walk.

4. Mom and Dad sometimes _____ the newspaper.

. You never _____ me what you want to eat.

5. My brother _____ everyone's cups after we eat breakfast.

Name _____ Date _____

From Farm to Market

Grammar Rules Present Tense Verbs	
Tell what one person or thing does now.	Use *s* at the end of the verb.
*Marta sel**ls** fruit.*	

Read each sentence. Circle the correct word. Write the word.

1. The farm ___grows___ flowers.   grow
   grows

2. Leo and Rita _____ flowers.   grow
   grows

3. The woman _____ flowers.   sell
   sells

4. Kyle and Eva _____ flowers.   sell
   sells

5. Mom _____ flowers.   buy
   buys

6. Andy and Jorge _____ flowers.   buy
   buys

Make a list of verbs with a partner. Write a sentence with one verb for your partner to read aloud.

Phonics

Words with <u>ch</u>, <u>tch</u>

<u>ch</u>in

Circle the word that names the picture.
Read and answer the question.

1. mask mast (match)	**2.** chap chest catch
3. batch bash bench	**4.** past pats patch
5. drink chin win	**6.** crutch crust club

Read It Together   Do you put a patch on pants or a bench?

Name _____ Date _____

Identify Details

Complete the Idea Web. Place one answer to the question in each circle.

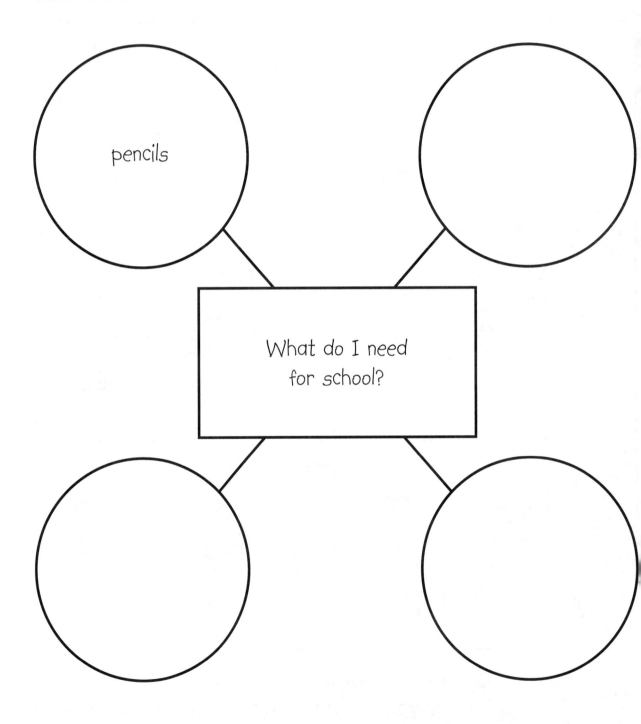

pencils

What do I need for school?

Name _____ Date _____

Use *Am* and *Are*

1. Get a marker. Take turns with a partner.

2. Put your marker on a pronoun—**I**, **we**, or **you**.

3. Slide your marker to a verb—**am** or **are**.

4. Can you make a sentence? Get one point.
   (Hint: I am _____ . We are _____ . You are _____ .)

5. Now your partner gets a turn.

6. Play until both partners make five sentences.

are	am	are	am	are	am
I	**We**	**You**	**We**	**I**	**You**

Phonics

Words with <u>ch</u>, <u>tch</u>

Write the letters to complete the word. Read and answer the question.

1.

chain

2.

ick

3.

in

4.

cru

5.

pea

6.

ma

Read It Together   Can a chick sit on a bench?

Name _____ Date _____

Blend Words

Circle the word that names the picture. Read and answer the question.

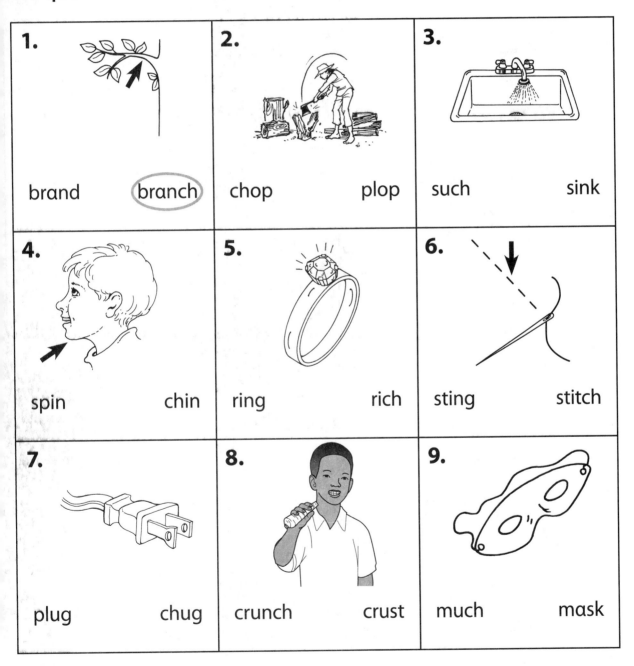

1. brand （branch）

2. chop   plop

3. such   sink

4. spin   chin

5. ring   rich

6. sting   stitch

7. plug   chug

8. crunch   crust

9. much   mask

Read It Together How much of the branch will he chop up?

Handwriting

High Frequency Words

Trace each word two times and then write it.

around around around

be be be

here here here

need need need

together together

together

where where where

Word Cards: *ch, tch, th*

lunch	watch	cloth	chick
chop	thump	hatch	thick
thing	chill	ranch	that
pitch	check	catch	such
path	itch	patch	with
chest	rich	chat	witch
batch	chin	math	much

High Frequency Word Cards

does	around
eat	be
live	here
no	need
see	together
why	where

For use with TE p. T161i   **PM3.35**   Unit 3 | To Your Front Door

Phonics

Words with <u>th</u>

Circle the word that names the picture. Read the sentence.

1.
(think)
sink
drink

2.
chin
thin
tin

3.
pan
that
path

4.
band
bath
bank

5.
then
test
tent

6.
tank
thank
than

Read It Together Thad can thank Ruth for this.

Name _____ Date _____

Fetch It!

Look at the picture. Write a word from the box to complete each sentence. Read the sentence.

High Frequency **Words**
around
be
here
need
together
where

_____

- - - - - - - - - - - - - - - - - - -

1. My dogs and I are at the pond _____ .

_____

- - - - - - - - - - - - - - - - - - -

2. I toss a stick, and they _____ to find it.

_____

- - - - - - - - - - - - - - - - - - -

3. My dogs sniff all _____ . They can not find the stick!

_____

- - - - - - - - - - - - - - - - - - -

4. _____ can the stick be?

_____

- - - - - - - - - - - - - - - - - - -

5. Look! It is _____ in the sand by the big rock!

Name _____ Date _____

Words with <u>th</u>

Write the letters to complete each word. Read and answer the questions.

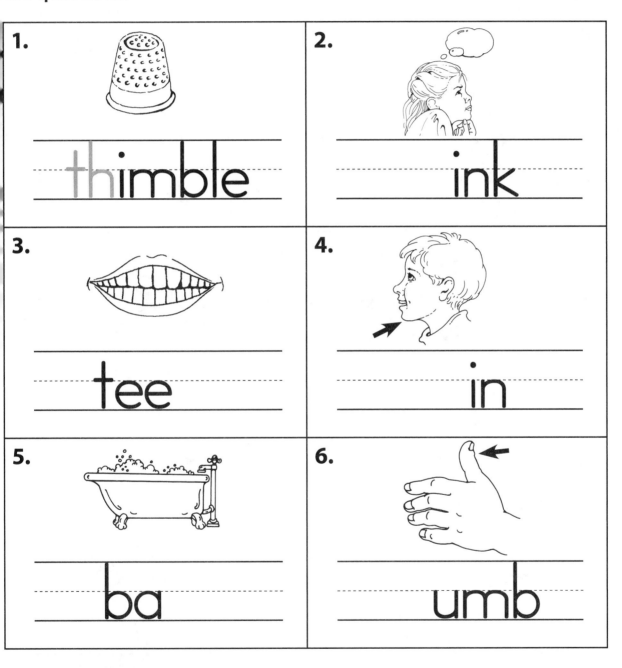

1. th imble

2. ___ ink

3. ___ tee

4. ___ in

5. ba ___

6. umb ___

Read It Together Does a dog want a bath? What do you think?

Phonics

Blend Words

Circle the word that names the picture. Read and answer the question.

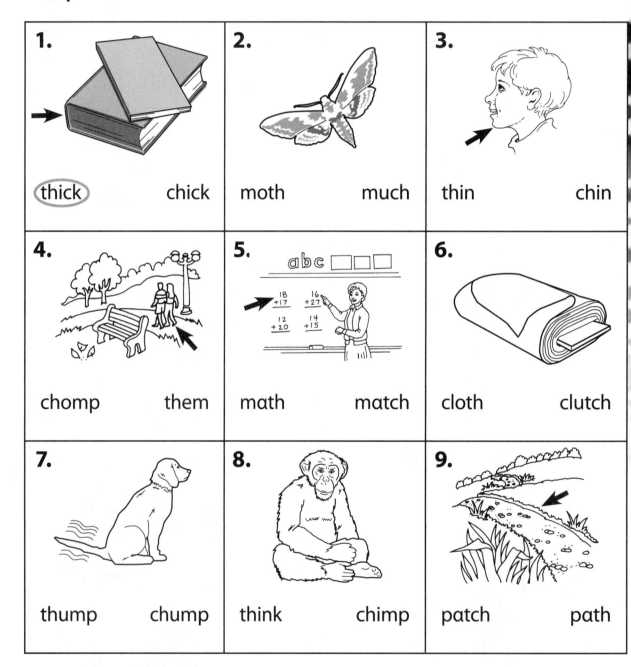

1. (thick) chick	**2.** moth much	**3.** thin chin
4. chomp them	**5.** math match	**6.** cloth clutch
7. thump chump	**8.** think chimp	**9.** patch path

Read It Together   Do you think that math is fun?

PM3.39

Be and the Present Progressive

1. **Read the words in the box.**

2. **Then read the letter.**

3. **Write the words that correctly complete the sentences in the letter.**

4. **Use each word only once.**

are sitting	is waving	are
is saying	am writing	is

Dear Uncle Nick,

I __am writing__ to you today from summer camp. Camp

_____ a lot of fun. We work in the garden and learn about

food every day. My best friends here _____ Ann and Tess.

Right now, we _____ under a big tree near our cabin.

Ann _____ to you and Tess _____

hello. See you soon.

Love,

Ella

Name _____ Date _____

Vocabulary Bingo

1. Write Key Words on the lines.

2. Listen to the clues. Place a marker on the Key Word.

3. Say "Bingo" when you have four markers in a row.

_____ _____ _____ _____

_____ _____ _____ _____

_____ _____ _____ _____

_____ _____ _____ _____

Idea Web

Delivery

Complete the Idea Web using details from "Delivery."

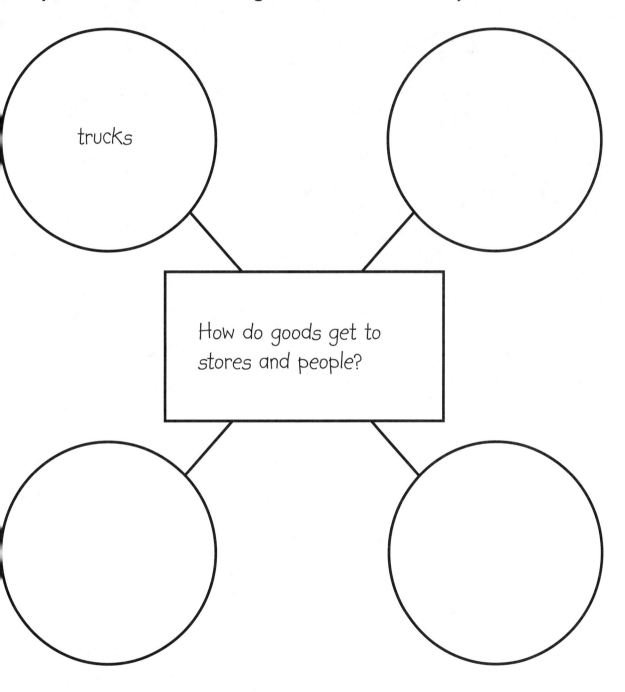

trucks

How do goods get to
stores and people?

💬 **Use your Idea Web to retell the poem to a partner.**

Phonics

Words with <u>wh</u>

Circle the word that names the picture. Read and answer the question.

1. thank, check, (whack)	**2.** chin, when, thin
3. whisk, thick, chuck	**4.** chip, whip, with
5. which, chick, think	**6.** whiff, cliff, fifth

Read It Together   Do you use a whiff or a whisk when you mix?

Phonics

Words with <u>wh</u>

Write the letters to complete the word. Read and answer the question.

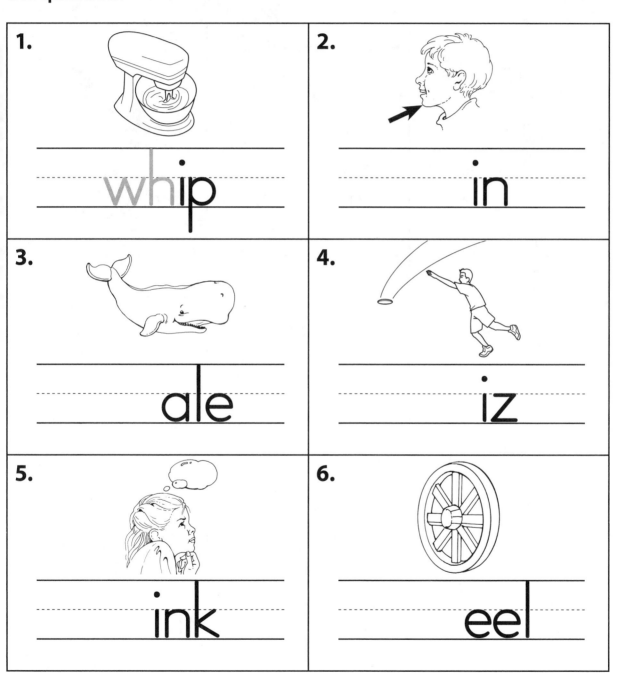

1. wh ip

2. ___ in

3. ___ ale

4. ___ iz

5. ___ ink

6. ___ eel

Read It Together What can you see whiz by when you go out?

Phonics

Blend Words

Circle the word that names the picture. Read and answer the question.

1. think whisk

2. which chimp

3. check what

4. with whip

5. thank when

6. whim whiff

7. wham chat

8. whack wing

9. chop whiz

Read It Together   What can you whack with a bat?

Name _____   Date _____

High Frequency Words

Trace each word two times and then write it.

come come come

found found found

full full full

next next next

their their their

walk walk walk

Word Cards: *wh, sh*

whiff	ship	whale	shell
shy	whisk	why	shack
should	shin	which	where
mush	whim	she	whip
when	shall	wash	whomp
shed	what	wham	shop
wheel	shawl	whiz	dish

High Frequency Word Cards

all	come
are	found
by	full
first	next
more	their
there	walk

Name _____ Date _____

Compare Genres

Compare a poem and a fact sheet.

Poem	Fact Sheet
has illustrations or pictures	has photographs

 Tell a partner how a poem and a fact sheet are different. Use your T-chart.

ship

Phonics

Words with <u>sh</u>

Circle the word that names the picture. Read the tongue twister.

1.

shop (circled)

chip

sip

2.

broth

brush

brick

3.

bash

bath

batch

4.

thud

when

shed

5.

shelf

whiff

self

6.

ditch

dust

dash

Read It Together   She put shells on the shelf in the shop.

Name _____ Date _____

What Did I Find?

Write a word from the box to complete each sentence. Guess the answer to the riddle.

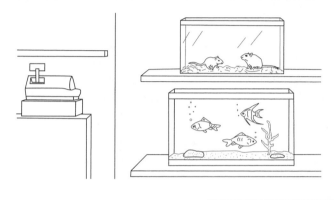

High Frequency **Words**
come
found
full
next
their
walk

_____

1. Come and see what I _____ in the shop!

2. They have no legs, but you can see

_____

_____ fins.

_____

3. They can swim, but they can not _____ .

_____

4. This tank is _____ of them.

_____

5. My _____ pet will be one of them.
What are they?

_____

Grammar: Verb: *Have*

Use *Have* and *Has*

Grammar Rules Verbs: have

Some verbs tell what the subject of a sentence has.

Subject	*Have*
I, you, or more than one person or thing	Use *have*.
one other person or thing	Use *has*.

1. Play One, Two, Three. Choose a word in Row 1.

2. Choose the verb that matches in Row 2.

3. Complete the sentence with a phrase from Row 3.

4. Take turns with a partner.

Row 1			
Marcus	I	Julio and Sara	Karen

Row 2			
has	has	have	have

Row 3			
a truck.	a plane.	a train.	a van.

 Read your sentences to a partner.

PM3.52

Name _____ Date _____

Words with <u>sh</u>

Write the letters to complete the word. Read the sentence.

1.

_____ ship

2.

_____ fi _____

3.

_____ ick

4.

_____ ell

5.

_____ ain

6.

_____ di _____

Read It Together   See the fish swim around the shell!

Blend Words

Circle the word that names the picture. Read and answer the question.

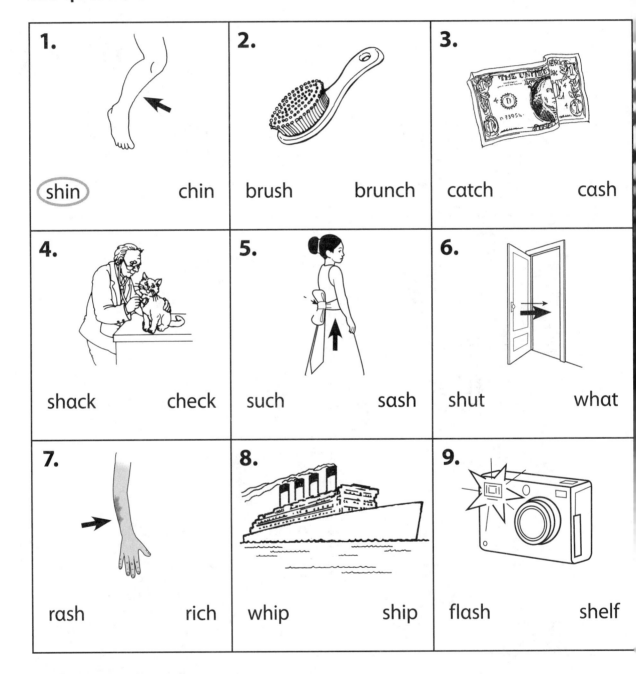

1. (shin)   chin

2. brush   brunch

3. catch   cash

4. shack   check

5. such   sash

6. shut   what

7. rash   rich

8. whip   ship

9. flash   shelf

Read It Together What do you shop for when you have cash?

Name _____ Date _____

Write Forms of *Have* and *Be*

Present Tense Verbs		Contractions
has	am	I'm
have	is	he's, she's, it's
	are	you're, they're

Look at the paragraphs. Write the missing words in the blanks. Use words from the chart.

My uncle _____is_____ a farmer. He _____

_____ a huge tractor. _____ as tall as my house!

Farmers _____ hard workers. Sometimes

_____ up at 4 o'clock in the morning.

_____ glad I do not get up at 4 a.m.!

Name _____ Date _____

Who Is? Who Has?

Grammar Rules Subject-Verb Agreement

Subject	To be	To have
one person or thing	is	has
more than one person or thing	are	have

Look at each picture below. Choose the correct verb in ( ) and write it on the line.

1. This _____ is _____ Tim. (is, are)

2. Lara _____ a cart. (have, has)

3. The children _____ hungry. (is, are)

4. Max and Sue _____ food. (have, has)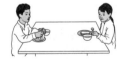

5. Max and Sue _____ full. (am, are)

Choose a form of *be* or *have*. Ask a partner to say a sentence using it.

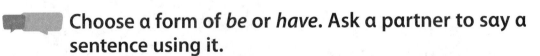

Name _____ Date _____

Idea Web

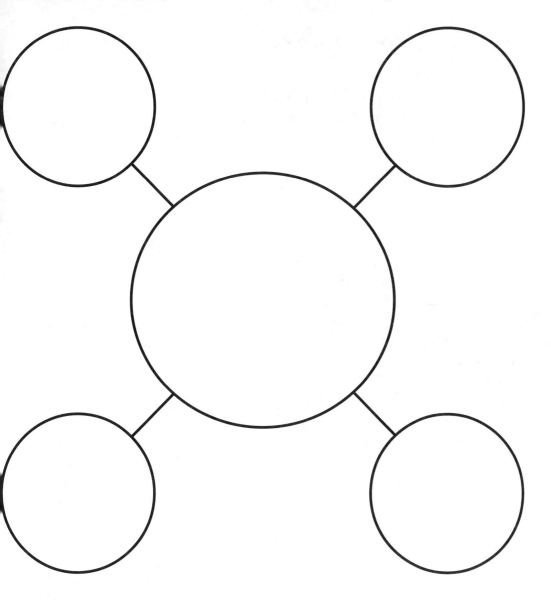

Voice Checklist

✓ Did you pick expressive words?
✓ Does your writing sound like you?
✓ Does your writing sound real?
✓ Do your words say what you want?

Name _____ Date _____

Words with Long <u>a</u>

c<u>a</u>ke

Circle the word that names each picture.

1. rack (rake) rat	**2.** lane lamp long
3. game gas gum	**4.** bell bake bed
5. cape cat cut	**6.** got get gate
7. tap tape tack	**8.** wave wax well

Read It Together Take the rake to the gate.

Name _____ Date _____

Identify Plot

Think of a story you know. Write or draw the plot in the chart.

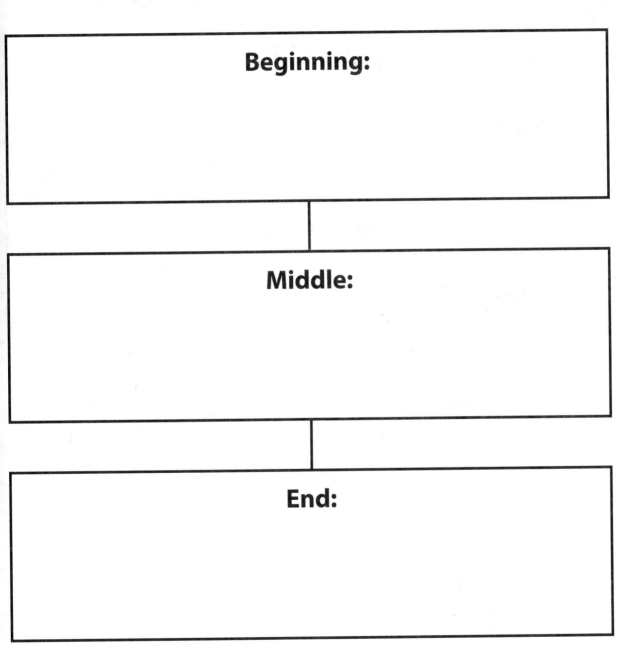

Beginning:

Middle:

End:

Name _____ Date _____

Blend Words

Circle the word that names each picture.

1.  (cape)　　　cake	**2.** 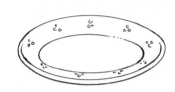 brake　　　plate	**3.**  grape　　　mane
4.  cane　　　wave	**5.** 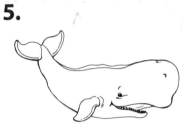 scale　　　whale	**6.**  skate　　　same
7.  date　　　snake	**8.**  save　　　flake	**9.**  frame　　　plane

Read It Together　Would a whale or a snake be in a lake?

Name _____ Date _____

Words with Long <u>a</u>

Complete each word so it names the picture.

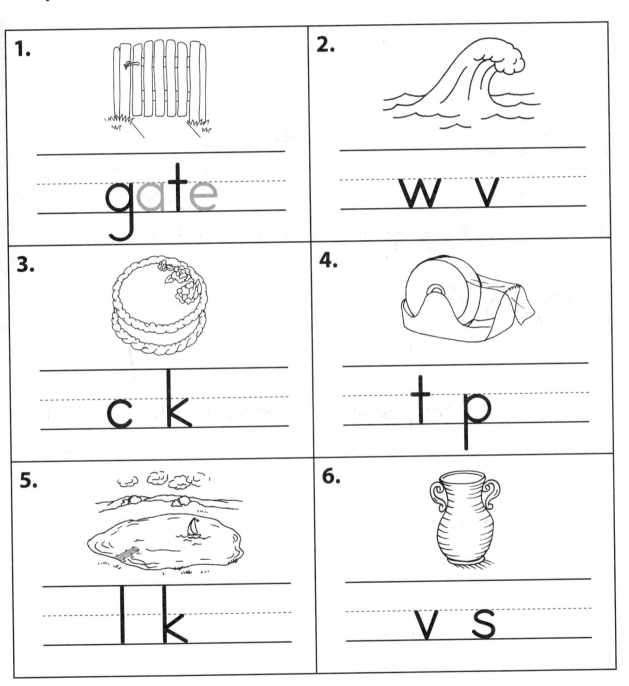

1. g a t e

2. w _ v _

3. _ c _ k _

4. t _ p _

5. _ l _ k _

6. v _ s _

Read It Together   Look at the waves in the lake.

Handwriting

High Frequency Words

Trace each word two times and then write it.

because because

because

carry carry carry

carry

don't don't don't don't

new new new

play play play

sleep sleep sleep

Long <u>a</u> Word Cards

snake	cane	game	gate
crate	bake	came	same
flame	cake	date	late
tame	wake	rake	mate
lane	lake	fame	rate
mane	flake	frame	plate
pane	take	plane	make

High Frequency Word Cards

go

because

great

carry

one

don't

saw

new

want

play

would

sleep

For use with TE p. T199k

Unit 4 | Growing and Changing

Name _____ Date _____

Contractions

| what + is = what's |
| is + not = isn't |

Read the sentences. Write the contraction for the underlined words.

1. Can you see <u>what is</u> in the pond?

_____

Can you see _____ in the pond?

2. I <u>can not</u> see a cat in the pond.

_____

I _____ see a cat in the pond.

3. It <u>is not</u> a cat.

_____

It _____ a cat.

4. I think <u>it is</u> a fish!

_____

I think _____ a fish!

High Frequency Words

What's in the Box?

Write a word from the box to complete each sentence.

High Frequency Words
because
carry
don't
new
play
sleep

1. Jack and Beth _____ have a dog.

2. They _____ with Gramps's dog.

3. They help Gramps _____ a box because it is big.

4. What's in the box? A _____ pup is in it!

5. They will play. Then the pup will _____ .

Word Cards: Subject Pronouns

I	you 大	he	she
it	we	you (more than one) 大大	they
duck	Dad	you and your sister	Dave
eggs	Ali and I	Mom	pond
my cousins and I	duckling	desk	myself
pencils	you and your brothers	Ana	yourself

Name _____ Date _____

Contractions

she + is	=	she's
did + not	=	didn't

Read the sentences. Write the contraction for the underlined words.

1. I <u>did not</u> see Jane. Did you?

_____

I _____ see Jane. Did you?

2. <u>She is</u> on the track.

_____

_____ on the track.

3. Jake <u>was not</u> on the track.

_____

Jake _____ on the track.

4. I think <u>he is</u> at bat.

_____

I think _____ at bat.

Grammar and Writing

Write Subject Pronouns

One	More Than One
I	we
you	you
he (for a male)	they
she (for a female)	they
it (for a thing or place)	they

Look at each pair of sentences. Look at the <u>underlined words</u> in the first sentence. Write the correct pronoun in the second sentence.

1. <u>Maya and Janet</u> look at the ducklings. _____ look at them every day.

2. <u>Maya</u> feeds the ducklings. _____ feeds them bread.

3. <u>Richard</u> walks around the pond. _____ walks quickly.

4. The <u>pond</u> is big. _____ is the ducks' home. [anno:] It

5. <u>My friend and I</u> watch the ducklings, too. _____ are happy to see them grow.

6. <u>You and your sister</u> must be quiet! _____ might scare the ducklings away.

Name _____ Date _____

Vocabulary Bingo

1. Write a Key Word in each egg.

2. Listen to the clues. Place a marker on the Key Word.

3. Say "Bingo" when you have four markers in a row.

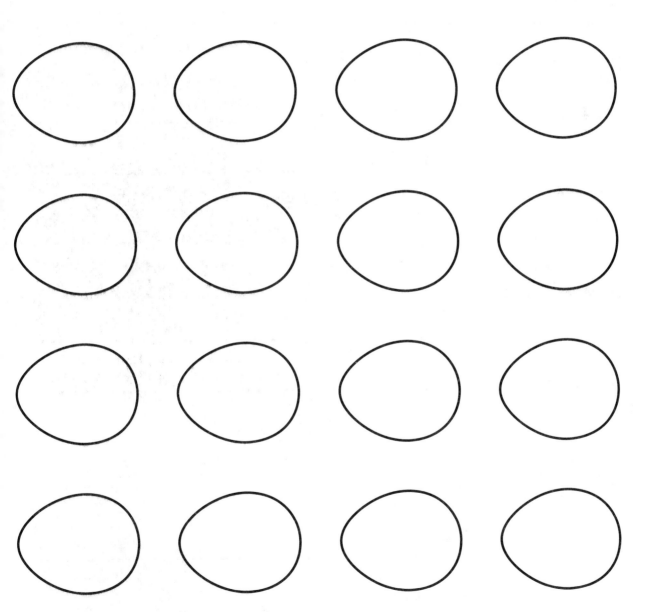

Name _____ Date _____

Ruby in Her Own Time

**Complete the chart. Write the important parts
of the plot from the story.**

Beginning:

First, Ruby hatches from an egg.

Middle:

End:

 **Use your chart to retell the story. Act out the events in order
to a partner.**

Name _____   Date _____

Words with Long i

k<u>i</u>te

Circle the word that names each picture.

1. fin fan (five)	**2.** back bake bike
3. lime lip lamp	**4.** dive date desk
5. date dime dim	**6.** name nine nest
7. him hale hive	**8.** bite bib brake

Read It Together   Would you like five dimes or five limes?

PM4.15   **Unit 4** | Growing and Changing

Grammar

The Pronoun Game

1. Make a spinner.
2. Play with a partner.
3. Take turns spinning the spinner.
4. Say a sentence with the pronoun.

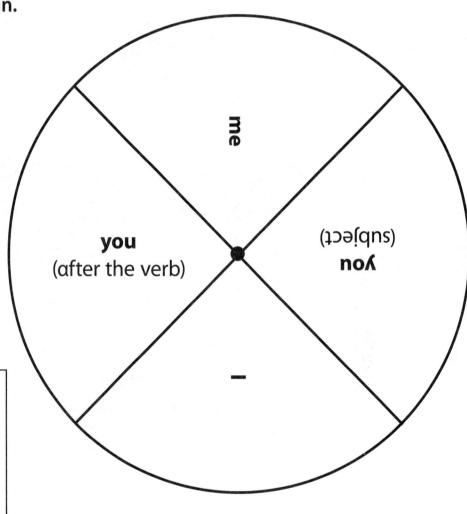

Make a Spinner

1. Put a paper clip ⊂⊃ in the center of the circle.

2. Hold one end of the paper clip with a pencil.

3. Spin the paper clip around the pencil.

Name _____   Date _____

Phonics

Blend Words

Circle the word that names the picture.

1. 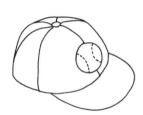 tap (tape)	**2.**  rid ride	**3.**  can cane
4.  cap cape	**5.** dim dime	**6.**  pin pine
7.  hat hate	**8.** 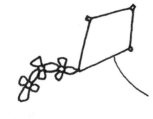 kit kite	**9.**  man mane

Read It Together Can a man ride a kite or a bike?

Name _____ Date _____

Words with Long i

Complete each word so it names the picture.

1. d i m e	**2.** d __ t
3. f __ v	**4.** k __ t
5. v __ s	**6.** h __ v

Read It Together   Give me the kite and five dimes.

Handwriting

High Frequency Words

Trace each word two times and then write it.

almost almost almost

both both both

kind kind kind

over over over

two two two

was was was

Long i Word Cards

bride	pile	time	five
smile	slide	dive	slide
mime	stride	hive	slime
hide	glide	hide	dime
file	tile	tide	thrive
wide	side	ride	strive
while	lime	drive	mile

High Frequency Word Cards

give	almost
he	both
know	kind
said	over
watch	two
who	was

For use with TE p. T233g   **PM4.21**   **Unit 4** | Growing and Changing

Name _____ Date _____

Compare Genres

Compare a story and a science article.

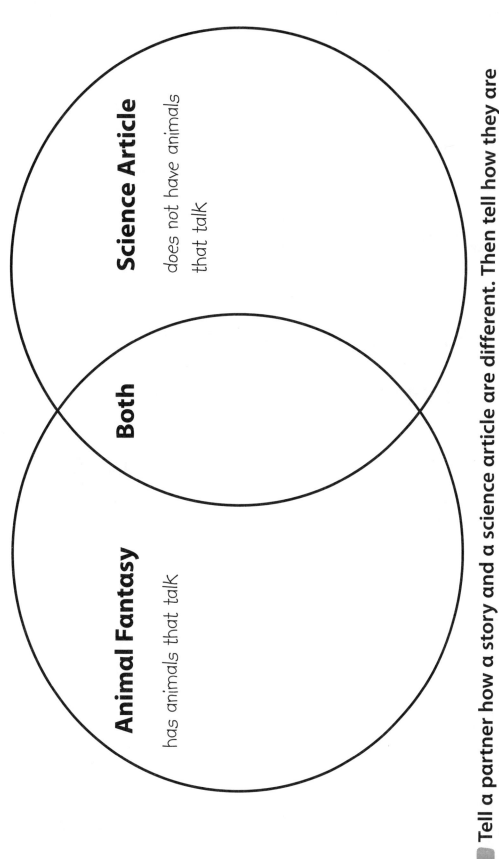

Science Article

does not have animals that talk

Both

Animal Fantasy

has animals that talk

Tell a partner how a story and a science article are different. Then tell how they are the same.

For use with TE p. T239g

PM4.22

Unit 4 | Growing and Changing

me	you	him
her	it	them
turtle	Dad	Paul
eggs	ocean	Mom
egg	nests	yourself
turtles	myself	Mara

Name _____   Date _____

Ending -<u>ed</u>

| grin + n + ed = grinned |
| bake – e + ed = baked |

Add the ending -*ed* to each word and write the new word.

grin
_____
- - - - - - - - - - - - - - - - -
1. He _____ .

bake
_____
- - - - - - - - - - - - - - - - -
2. He _____ .

clap
_____
- - - - - - - - - - - - - - - - -
3. She _____ .

smile
_____
- - - - - - - - - - - - - - - - -
4. He _____ .

Phonics
Ending -<u>ing</u>

run + n + ing = running
bake − e + ing = baking

Add the ending -ing to each word and write the new word.

jog

_____

- -

1. He is _____ .

dive

_____

- -

2. She is _____ .

swim

_____

- -

3. She is _____ .

wave

_____

- -

4. He is _____ .

Name _____ Date _____

At Bat

Write a word from the box to complete each sentence.

High Frequency **Words**
almost
both
kind
over
two
was

_____

1. Stan _____ at bat.

_____

2. He had _____ strikes.

_____

3. The pitch came. It was the _____ Stan liked.

_____

4. He hit it up _____ all the kids and almost out!

_____

5. _____ Mom and Dad clapped.

Name _____ Date _____

Write Pronouns

Subject	After the Verb
I	me
you	you
he	him
she	her
it	it
they	them

Look at each pair of sentences. Look at the <u>underlined words</u> in the first sentence. Write the correct pronoun in the second sentence.

1. Dave, Joe, and Ana watch <u>the turtles</u>. They watch ___them___ every day.

2. <u>Dave, Joe, and Ana</u> want to help them. _____ decide to feed them.

3. Dave feeds <u>one turtle</u>. He feeds _____ too much.

4. <u>Joe</u> meets <u>Dave</u> on the beach. _____ meets _____ at 4 p.m.

5. Joe sees <u>Ana</u> on the beach. He sees _____ on the sand.

6. <u>I</u> can't use all the turtle food. Please don't give _____ any more.

Name _____ Date _____

Ending -<u>ed</u>

Circle the word that completes each sentence and write it.

hugged **hiked**

_____

1. Zane _____ up the path.

lugged **liked**

_____

2. He _____ to sing.

hummed **hated**

_____

3. He _____ a song as he walked.

jogged **jabbed**

_____

4. Jen _____ by Zane.

chopped **chimed**

_____

5. She _____ in and sang with him.

Phonics

Ending -ing

Circle the word that completes each sentence and write it.

shopping   shining

1. The sun is _____ .

robbing   riding

2. Shane is _____ his bike on the path.

running   raking

3. Meg is _____ next to him.

chopping   chasing

4. Matt is _____ them on his skates.

stopping   sliding

5. Are the pals _____ to have a snack?

Name _____ Date _____

The Make-It-a-Pronoun Game

Grammar Rules Subject Pronouns

Use *I* for yourself.	<u>I</u> draw a turtle.
Use *he* for a male.	<u>Jun</u> draws a turtle. <u>He</u> draws a turtle
Use *she* for a female.	<u>Aida</u> draws a turtle. <u>She</u> draws a turtle.
Use *they* for more than one person.	<u>Jun and Aida</u> draw turtles. <u>They</u> draw turtles.

1. **Play with a partner.**
2. **Spin the spinner.**
3. **Change the noun to a subject pronoun.**

Make a Spinner

1. Put a paper clip ⊂⊃ in the center of the circle.

2. Hold one end of the paper clip with a pencil.

3. Spin the paper clip around the pencil.

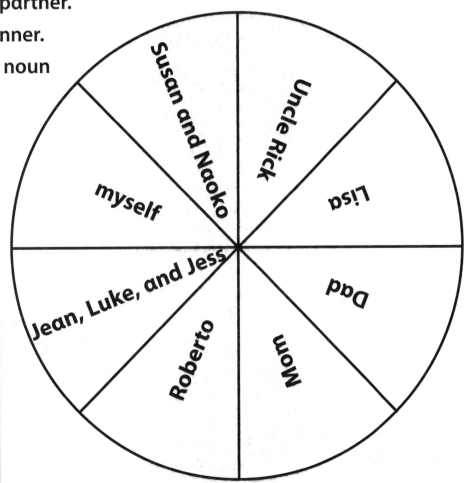

Phonics

Words with Long o

<u>rope</u>

Circle the word that names each picture.

1.		2.	
	not (nose) name		hate hat hose

3.		4.	
	cone cane can		rake rack robe

5.		6.	
	name nap not		box bone band

7.		8.	
	run rock rose		hot home hand

Read It Together   The hose is by the roses at home.

For use with TE p. T241q   **PM4.31**   **Unit 4** | Growing and Changing

Name _____   Date _____

Identify Main Idea and Details

Choose an animal. Write details about how the animal changes as it grows.

Main Idea: _____ change as they grow.

Detail:

Detail:

Detail:

Phonics

Words with Long <u>o</u>

Complete each word so it names the picture.

1. _____ n o t e	**2.** _____ c ___ n
3. _____ t ___ p	**4.** _____ r ___ s
5. 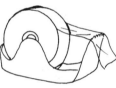 _____ n ___ s	**6.**  _____ v ___ s

Read It Together Smell the rose with your nose.

Name _____ Date _____

Words with <u>ph</u>

<u>ph</u>one

Complete each word so it names the picture.

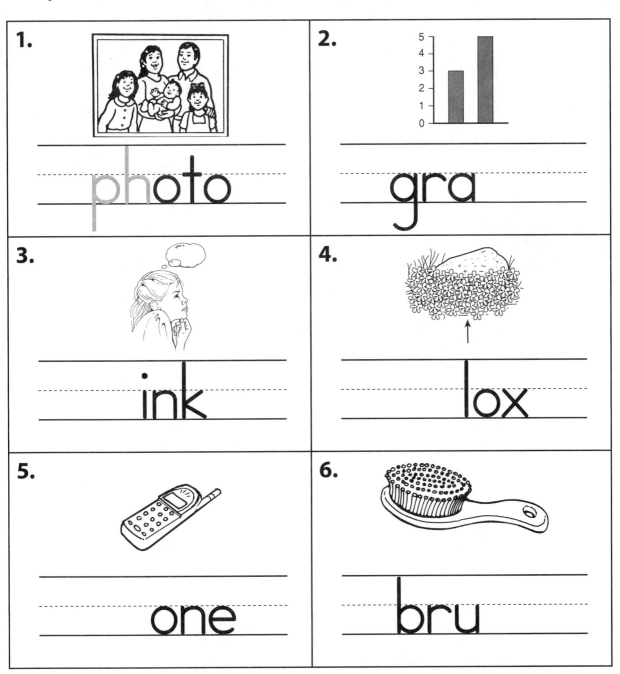

1. <u>ph</u>oto

2. gra_____

3. _____ink

4. _____lox

5. _____one

6. bru_____

Read It Together   Would you see a graph or phlox by the rocks?

For use with TE p. T244f   **PM4.34**   **Unit 4** | Growing and Changing

Name _____ Date _____

High Frequency Words

Trace each High Frequency Word two times and then write it.

always always always

any any any

each each each

every every every

many many many

never never never

Long o Word Cards

cold	hole	bone	hose
nose	cone	gold	hold
close	pole	stone	phone
sold	rose	mold	bold
stole	pose	zone	mole
fold	role	shone	those
told	whole	lone	zone

High Frequency Word Cards

around	always
be	any
here	each
need	every
together	many
where	never

Name _____ Date _____

Story Map

Beginning:

Middle:

End:

Organization Checklist

✓ Does the story have a beginning?
✓ Does the story have a middle?
✓ Does the story have an end?
✓ Are there words that signal the beginning, middle, and end?